Finding the Words

For Roxie —
Finally!
Thanks for your help.

Nancy.

FINDING
THE WORDS

Conversations With
Writers Who Teach

Nancy L. Bunge

SWALLOW PRESS
Athens Ohio   Chicago   London
OHIO UNIVERSITY PRESS

Swallow Press books are published
by Ohio University Press, Athens, Ohio 45701

Library of Congress Cataloging in Publication Data
Bunge, Nancy L.

Finding the words.

1. English language–Rhetoric–Study and teaching.
2. Creative writing–Study and teaching. 3. Authors,
American–20th century–Interviews. 4. College teachers
–United States–Interviews. 5. Authors as teachers.
I. Title.
PE1404.B78   1984   808'.042   84-8544
ISBN 0-8040-0861-2
ISBN 0-8040-0862-0 (pbk.)

Contents

Preface

These sixteen interviews took place during the three years I spent interviewing some fifty writer-teachers. I set out intending to gather discussions of the writer's growing involvement in university life, and I did; but on the way, I heard fascinating explanations of the way one teaches and learns how to write. I decided to make this information available to the many who could use it by collecting those interviews which best illuminate the writing process.

My work rests on the kindness of many people. I owe an obvious debt to all the writers I spoke with, and their generosity extended far beyond what appears on the page. I could not have begun without a sabbatical leave and a research initiation grant from the Michigan State University. As I perservered, many people helped me along with good advice, including David Anderson, Henry Bredeck, Mike Colleran, Robert Combs, Bruce Cook, Macel Ezell, Ralph Kron, Roxie Fuller McLean, Henry Silverman, Steve Wilbers, David Wright, Robert Wright, and, especially, Paul Ferlazzo. This was a fine project for someone with lots of money and nerve. Since I have little of either, I needed and got encouragement, food, and shelter from old friends along my route: Jackie and Peter Allaman, Jay and Zee Claiborne, Patti Davis, Sheila Friedling, Sharon Furrow, Marc and Ellen Green, Linda and Jim Sherwood, and Margaret Sullivan. The book also demanded long hours at the typewriter; fortunately, Merrilyn Wenner was generous with her enthusiasm as well as her typing expertise. I doubt that this project would have occurred to me if I had not had excellent teachers over the years. Those who have come to mind most persistently during the past three years are: Merton M. Sealts, Jr., the late Harry Hayden Clark, my brother, my parents, and my students.

This is a good chance to thank all these people for everything in the book that may have value. I made the mistakes by myself.

Grateful acknowledgement is made to the following authors, publishers and journals for permission to reprint previously published materials.

American Poetry Review for "An Interview with William Stafford," Vol. 10, No. 6 (1981), and for "The University Is Something Else You Do," an interview with Marvin Bell, Vol. 11, No. 2. (1982).

San Francisco Review of Books for "An Interview with Clarence Major," Vol. 7, No. 3. (1982).

Teachers & Writers Collaborative for "An Interview with Clarence Major," from *The Point Where Teaching and Writing Intersect,* edited by Nancy Larsen Shapiro and Ron Padgett. Copyright © 1983.

Introduction

Since American education supposedly offers everyone a chance to guarantee a reservation for the good life, when test scores indicate that American children do not write well, the media shudders, parents concerned with "accountability" storm PTA meetings, and teachers concentrate on areas of instruction certain to appear on the Test. The assumption behind this uproar, that those who get high test scores will later become rich and consequently lead happy lives, makes little sense, but Americans are too busy pursuing the American Dream to question it. In their haste to make it, many fail to notice that they confuse the appearance of achievement with genuine contentment for a lifetime.

Because skills have more market value and greater visibility than ideas, American education has become vocational. Ben Franklin showed us how to do it. He taught himself to write in much the same way that he might have trained a socially ambitious bear to dance the minuet, relying heavily on repetition and imitation to develop a polite style with the appearance of culture, the appearance of wisdom, and the appearance of humility. Franklin passes on his winning approach in a stylistically polished, conceptually incoherent and ethically dubious autobiography. We still use Franklin's techniques just as we still embrace the tenets of his distinctly American faith; we continue to believe that "early to bed, early to rise, makes a man healthy, wealthy, and wise," that every problem has a clear, direct solution, and that writing is a skill anyone can develop with a series of mechanical exercises.

Teachers across the land order their students to get out a piece of paper for a spelling test, smug in the knowledge that this return to the basics will make their students write well; adults eagerly complete the exercises in the latest book that promises to teach them to write beautifully in twelve easy lessons; scholars confidently produce unreadable descriptions of teaching methods guaranteed to quickly transform class-rooms of marginally literate students into fluent writers. Like Franklin, we know that good writing comes from using good techniques to discipline ourselves into good habits. As we reassure each other in this faith, American writing deteriorates.

Casualties of the Ben Franklin school appear in my expository writing classes each fall. Convinced by armies of resolute teachers that they will write well only when they learn to ignore their own judgment and obey the rules, these reasonable, pleasant human beings struggle to kill off their healthy resistance to the misguided edicts of well-intentioned writing teachers: "Never ask a question!" "Never express an opinion!" "Never get personal!" "Never use 'I'!" In other words, convince the reader you are an omniscient robot. This approach not only violates the students, who are, after all, human beings; it does not work.

I set out to interview writer-teachers hoping to collect teaching techniques. I quickly learned that since they do not believe in training people to write, they have few surefire exercises to pass on. Instead they talk about honesty. Of course, they recommend that their students read widely and work hard; but they all believe that good writing finally depends on having the integrity to see honestly, the compassion to accept what one sees, and the courage to express it clearly. Perhaps one can write dishonestly and win prizes, or even help found a country; but one who operates this way has certainly lost some internal rewards and perhaps even damaged some talent. Consequently, they teach writing, but not how to write a best-seller because they believe that one learns to write well not by mastering a skill or an audience, but by accepting oneself. Practice does perfect, but since the inner life of writing comes from the inner life of the writer, the successful writing teacher encourages students to rest in and write from themselves.

As their interviews show, these writers do this in different ways; but I think they are their own best instructional models. Their classes shape themselves around the students' response to each other's work; this indicates to the students not only that their writing and their aesthetic judgments deserve serious consideration, but also that their spontaneous responses have value. This trust in the students must help the students trust themselves and each other. The classes I observed validated this confidence. The students used their freedom to do good work, pooling their energy and insight to clarify and heighten the best aspects of the writings discussed. The teachers either stood aside, allowing the students to discover things for themselves, or they joined the students in their expeditions. They never directed the class and certainly never announced any rules. Teaching such a class requires concentration, spontaneity, sensitivity, and confidence–all qualities essentail to serious writing. So these writers provide living examples of that vitality critical to writing well. Former students repeatedly identify this unconscious instruction in what it's like to *be* a writer as the most valuable part of their program, again certifying the indissolvable link between how one writes and how one is.

Because of this tie, the way these writers talk has at least as much value to the aspiring writer as what they say. Each interview takes its own direction. I hope their distinctness means I successfully adapted to each person I spoke with; I know that the differences between them reflect the integrity of the people I interviewed. These writers have useful advice for those who want to improve their writing, but the insight the interviews allow into the writers' personalities should educate those who read them in much the same way that the writers' presence educates their students.

I also hope that these interviews challenge the myth of the mad artist. When friends warned that pursuing this project would lead me into difficult encounters with overblown egos, I nodded knowingly. I had read my Freud and my Jung, so I knew that people pay for talent with neurosis. As these writers invited me into their homes, allowed me to ask anything I wanted, offered me food, rides, and advice, I had to question this stereotype. As I became aware that all these kindnesses reflected a trusting responsiveness to virtually everything and everyone, I stood my preconception on its head and concluded that talent thrives best in healthy human beings. Granted, I did interview a self-selected group of generous people. Since I had no contacts, I could do nothing but write or call, identify myself, describe my project, ask for their time, and hope. They did not disappoint me. And their benevolence persisted to the end: when they reviewed and approved the interviews for publication, the writers who made changes did not alter my rendition of our conversation, but polished rough edges beyond my reach.

When I asked them why they were so nice to me they would say it was because they liked the attention. But I don't think this explains their kindness as successfully as their own analysis of what makes a writer. As they told me, in order to write well one must cultivate spontaneity, and this in turn demands trust in oneself and in the world. And that generous hopefulness permeates the way these writers act, the way they talk, and the way they are. If they pass this on to their students, then they will have done something more significant and more inclusive than training their students to produce best-sellers. Freud and Jung notwithstanding, common sense approves those qualities which writers believe necessary to their craft and attempt to encourage in their students: honesty, spontaneity, and clarity. If they succeed, they have earned their wages and our respect.

The education these writers offer has little immediate pragmatic value, but a great deal of human value. Not surprisingly, they not only reject the Ben Franklin method of writing instruction, they also reject the American Dream that many people believe they exemplify. They talk of another American Dream, a dream of integrity and candor, and this is the dream they strive to help their students fulfill.

Finding the Words

MARVIN BELL

NB: What do you want your students to get from your classes?

MB: A sense of themselves and what the possibilities are for them. And *that* they find out partly by finding out what the possibilities are for poetry. I don't want them to write like me. I don't want them to think like me. I want them to go their own ways and toward that end I want them to be able to read their own work and see what it really is. At any given time one's poetry is a fair representation of what one's life's probably. . . . One always feels, "Oh, that's not me, that's not me, that's not me"; but really, that is you, that is you, that is you, and after a while that gets to be OK. That's the real leap people have to make in maturation. In maturing they begin to accept what they are and to actually work with what they are and to build on that. Now that's what I would like to encourage in my students. Absolutely. And some of them are able to begin that kind of essential work while they're still students. Others don't really get it until a few years later. I get a lot of letters.

NB: How do you encourage that? Do you have them keep journals?

MB: I don't require them to do anything, but I don't forbid anything either. I assume they're all men and women of some commitment and of some maturity, as they *are* here; they may not be quite like that everywhere in that they wouldn't be here if they weren't committed to writing.

NB: Then how do you encourage them to accept themselves?

MB: Well, I do several things. One is to insist on what the words are saying in class. We try to figure out exactly what's in the poem.

1

It may be of interest to us to know what the poet's intentions were and what else is behind the poem, but we also try to make it absolutely clear to one another what's there in the poem, what does it actually say, what do the sentences say. That's one thing—learning to read your words carefully. And another thing is to encourage them to be not only unlike me when they're writing, but unlike one another and to learn from the work that most threatens them, because the work that doesn't upset them is work that's like their own. Especially when one is young, that defensiveness gets in the way. When a poem is praised in class, it's so easy for everyone else who writes differently to say, "Uh oh, if that poem is good, then maybe the way I write is no good." Then learning stops and defensiveness takes over. So I try to encourage them to be unlike one another and to appreciate every different way of writing and to learn from what seems most alien to them, to read good work widely, to read their own work carefully, and to give themselves permission, permission to try anything, over and over, because one of the great secrets—I hope it's not really a secret—about writing, is that if you do anything seriously enough, long enough, you'll get better at it. Then some teachers try to take credit. *(Laughter.)*

NB: Is it a problem that your students have primarily literary backgrounds?

MB: They don't have backgrounds in other fields, but they have lots of other interests. Many of the students in the Workshop are a little older than they would be if they came here directly from undergraduate school, so that's one thing. Another thing is, they tend to be odd, interesting people who've always had a number of interests. We do try to encourage the students to get out of the Workshop milieu and out of the English Department for some of their courses. We think it'd be just terrific if people took paleontology, karate, and home economics, all of which would count toward their degree. But again, we can't really require it and it wouldn't work out if we did. We just rely on them wanting to know things. Generally, poets do want to know things. On the one hand, it's just wonderful for poets to, say, read books about insects. On the other hand, it doesn't make them experts. Ezra Pound in the *ABC of Reading* tells a story about Dempsey, the prize fighter, during the days when Tunney and Dempsey were both great fighters and people would talk about how intelligent Tunney was while Dempsey was not thought to be too intelligent. And so, Dempsey was asked about a novel that had prize fighting in it and he simply said, "It's not like that." So the person asking said, "Well, I see you're reading a novel about a Grand Duke of Russia. How do you know whether that's like that?" Dempsey said, "I never *wuz* a Grand Duke." And that applies to some extent to people who think that poets should be reading up on insects, say, and then mentioning insects in their next poem. It's one thing to know a little; it's another thing to really know.

NB: So good poetry is written out of . . .

MB: Nobody knows. Again, I think it's just wonderful for a poet to read a book on insects, or even one hundred books on insects, but . . . When black holes were discovered, there was suddenly a spate of poems about black holes. And these poems, as far as I could tell, never did anything except discover the black hole as a metaphor for whatever else they were going to say. And most of what they were going to say were the standard things: "I'm lonely," "I'm not lonely," "I hurt," "I don't hurt," "I want," "I don't want."

NB: I guess that's true. I thought that the more people knew, the better poetry they'd write; but you're right.

MB: In some cases, it's true. Poets do love to learn things that are of use and one of the best things about being a poet is that one can become more and more educated through one's art without going about it in an organized fashion. It's great to have subject matter and there are some people who have subject matter by virtue of how their lives have gone, in some cases quite horribly. On the other hand, Emily Dickinson's life was not very exciting except in her mind and even Whitman didn't cover the country in person as well as his poems did on the page.

NB: Is it a problem that more and more people are becoming poets by going to workshops rather than by riding around on steamers?

MB: On the great scale of human vices, writing a bad poem doesn't weigh very much. In any case, why should only people who can do something well be permitted to do it? That's crazy. If that's true, I should give up running because when I run a marathon, I finish so much after Bill Rogers or Frank Shorter that it isn't the same event. I like to point out to people that in the Honolulu Marathon last year, I passed Frank Shorter. Unfortunately, I was running one way and he was already doubling back toward the finish line. So what's the point? Who plays baseball in this country? Only the people who are going to make it to the major leagues? And who goes to the baseball games? The people who go to baseball games, those millions of people who attend professional baseball games every year, are people who either played baseball or are attending the game with someone who did; they have an interest in it and they have some knowledge of it because they've tried it themselves. Well, how can it hurt the best poetry for a lot of people to try it themselves? That's crazy. People who are against workshops essentially hate young people. That's all. They hate young people. They don't want any competition. They're elitists in the worst sense. There's a good sense of being elite which has to do with quality; but when one becomes elitist in terms of participation, that's a horrible position to take. There are academic paratroopers who drop in for a night and blast workshops, then they pick up their checks from the Workshop and they sell their books to the students, and they go on home. Some of us stay right here in the trenches.

NB: I meant that some people say it could be a problem that more and more poets come out of school and are, consequently, out of touch with the real world.

MB: Aaww, nobody comes out of school. That's absurd. A few years of college or a couple years of graduate school don't change your character. I grew up in a town where people don't go to college, where most people make their living, or did at the time, from duck farms, fishing, potato farms, and from small town activities. I went off to college wearing a leather jacket with a switch blade in my pocket because I didn't know any better. When I got there, I found out that nobody was wearing a leather jacket; as far as I could tell, they didn't have switch blades. Well now, I don't think my character was going to be changed by graduate school or even many years of undergraduate school then followed by graduate school. That's absurd. My character, even as it develops now, is undoubtedly based on things I do that have nothing to do with teaching as much as on my job, which is teaching. If people who go to the university are out of touch with reality, what happens to people who spend eight or ten hours a day on an automobile assembly line? There's a kind of romanticism among poets that says, "Oh, if you work in the mines, if you work in the factories, you're in the real world." That's non-sense. Nobody comes out of the university; the university is some-thing else you do. Even during the years one is in the university, does one give up all the passions and desires and activities and angers and hates and fears and so forth, that one has, because one is in the university, and start over? It might be good if we could, but we don't.

NB: In one interview you said that the students' fascination with technical facility used to pose a problem, but that it was going away. Then somewhere else you said that your students had to struggle against a world where no one has any respect for working hard at writing well.

MB: Well, tendencies come and go in the Workshop. It's hard to judge one class against another. But if one looks back to twenty years ago, when I was a student in the Workshop, one can see that the kind of poetry dominating the worksheets was different from the kind of poetry one sees on the worksheets now. Let me put it this way. The best poets are always the best poets. They're people who have the drive, the commitment, the need, whatever it is, to teach themselves or to learn from me and other people. It's always the second-best poets in whom one finds the regrettable tendencies of an age. When an anthology is published, for example, the reviews are always nega-tive, probably because the reviews are always written by people who aren't in the anthology and who are jealous. When you want to look for a way to put down an anthology or a workshop, it's very easy. You just ignore the best poems and the best poets, and you find, if you can, those regrettable tendencies in the second- and third-best poets. The best work is always so good that it escapes these consider-ations. It's always original, it's always unique, it's always personal, intimate.

I think a number of good things have happened in American poetry in the last twenty years and those events have influenced the work one sees everywhere, including the Workshop here. I think the old argument about free verse versus metered verse has exhausted itself. As a free verse poet, writing free verse from a long time back, I had to know everything I could know about meter, partly to defend myself and partly to be sure of what I was doing. I'm doing things in poetry which I think would not work well in meters and I don't write metered verse, but I think it's probably a help to a young poet's ear to know how to read metered verse if not how to write it. But there are grand theoretical questions about this. James Wright in the last book he published before his death, a book called *To a Blossoming Pear Tree,* includes a poem about Ralph Neal, the Scout Master in Martins Ferry, Ohio and it's a poem written in prose. In fact, it's a piece of prose, or is it? Nobody really knows or even cares to know any more. We've gotten past all that. "Poetry," which was for so long a word that had something to do with lines, and for some people also with meters, stanzas and verse forms, has in a sense returned to a more fundamental sense of the word which is very hard to pin down, but which has to do with the quality of the imagination and further, the quality of an imaginative engagement with the world or the subject matter. So someone will say about a piece of writing, "Oh, that's sheer poetry." And it would be easy to laugh and say, "Oh, they're just speaking from ignorance," but they're really not. They're speaking from a heartfelt understanding which is probably more accurate than all those technical definitions we used to apply. So the situation in poetry has changed. And there are many poets in this country, good poets, who still write very well in meters and rhyme who, I think, feel threatened and feel ignored by a young generation which in many respects doesn't know and doesn't care about meters and rhyme. Out of their feelings of being threatened, they have exaggerated the importance of meter and rhyme in poetry and they have then tried in desperate ways, I think, to prove to us that free verse is a kind of aberration and that the history of poetry will proceed mostly in terms of meters. And I think they're wrong.

I also think many kinds of images are showing up in poems now that didn't show up before, partly because of the influence of translation. In the fifties and even on into the sixties, the young poets in this country were bitterly rational. I think now there's less rationality and more passion. We've gained permission for our poetry from work translated from other cultures: all kinds of permission. It always was true and still is to some extent that people would see a poem translated by a Russian poet and they would say, "How Russian!" They'd see the same poem by an American poet and they'd say, "This is just self-indulgent, overly grand." Or they'd see a short poem by a Japanese poet and they'd say, "Oh, isn't this wonderful. How Japanese!" They'd see the same poem next to an American byline and they'd say, "How skimpy! How begrudging! How stingy!" They'd see a poem containing wonderful political ironies by an East European and they'd say, "Oh yes, this is the kind of wonderful poetry one gets out from behind the Iron Curtain." But they'd see the same poem written by an American poet and they'd say "Oh, how frivolous." So a lot of that prejudice has been weakened by our seeing so much good work in translation.

The poets in the Workshop are incredible talents. Although many of them will quit writing over the ten years after they leave here, they won't quit for lack of talent. They'll quit because they no longer need to. And when I read the theses each spring, I'm really amazed; I would say a good half of the theses are as good as, or better than, the better first books that are coming out that year. They're really that good. It's certainly much better than when I was a graduate student.

NB: What would have happened to you if you hadn't come here?

MB: Well, I've thought about that. I got married and had a child very early and then was divorced from my wife and kept the child, so I had to work and make a living and I don't know what would have happened. I was stalling the army. I had an old commission and I knew I was going to have to go on active duty eventually; I tried unsuccessfully many times in many ways to get out of it and couldn't. I stalled them over seven years, but I knew I'd have to go in eventually. So it was crucial to me to find a way of testing my commitment further and producing more work, really being able to think about the writing and do it, and that's what the Writing Workshop afforded me. That's what it affords everybody—a sense of community and a pervasive sense of commitment and time.

NB: You said that many other programs "have faculty members who feel too good about teaching writing, who feel that it's a credit to themselves, which is, I think, a bad way to feel." What did you mean?

MB: I think what I meant is that creating the right response in their students takes precedence over raising their standards. Remember *Marjorie Morningstar?*

NB: Vaguely.

MB: In the movie version Gene Kelly plays the big fish in the small pond where he is the music teacher, I guess, at an all-girls school, is it? I don't remember too well. Anyway, Marjorie discovers him and takes him to Broadway where, of course, he fails utterly. Marjorie tracks him down and finds him sitting at the piano playing to his adoring girl students just as he had at the beginning. Well, the big-fish-in-the-little-pond syndrome is common to artists in universities. In that regard, the best thing, I think, about Iowa City is that it is so common to be a poet or a writer of any kind or an artist of any kind here that it's impossible to keep pretending one is more special than one is. Everyone knows you fell down the stairs last week; everybody knows that you're human and I think that's healthy. The other half of this, of course, is that one does achieve a certain kind of confidence that one might not otherwise achieve by being paid attention to. That's a terrible thing to say perhaps, but I think it's true.

NB: Some people I've spoken with say that many writers stop producing when they teach because teaching depletes their creative energy.

MB: I think there's a very complicated psychological dynamic going on in teaching in that when teachers first begin to teach they really need to be liked by their students. And I think teaching can be a very interesting and strange and rich activity; it can also be endlessly tiring and thoroughly exhausting for the same reasons. It's a little like giving blood except that nobody turns the tap off unless you the teacher decide to turn it off yourself. That's one of the things that teachers have to learn to do — to turn the tap off, so they're not depleted of their own blood.

On the other hand, when anyone says that teaching interferes with their writing, I suspect that if it weren't teaching, it would be something else interfering with their writing. I go through long periods when I don't write and I can find many excuses, I can find many reasons for why I am not writing and I can rail against those obstructions to writing, but the truth is that when one really needs to write, one will find a way to do it.

NB: What did you mean when you said, "The academic life is dangerous to talent not because it is tame, but because it offers too many definitions. The academy trusts language almost without reservation. Writers who matter to us do not"?

MB: Yeah.

NB: You agree with that?

MB: Absolutely!

NB: What does it mean?

MB: *(Laughter.)* Well, it means that language can be misused and the more intelligent the person misusing it, the better they can misuse it. It's not just politicians coming up with words like "deniability," or "protective retaliatory strike," it's also the kind of nonsense that passes for Structuralism, and Post-structuralist theorizing and the sort of high-falutin' talk that goes on now in the name of semiotics and hermeneutics—Mr. Herman Neutics. And it's just nonsense, all that stuff. When language is pushed in a certain way, it loses logic. And I believe that I can go through the essays of the kind of critics I've just mentioned and I can show you where the logic breaks down. But obviously, not many people either can or want to do such a thing. Who would want to waste one's time on that? So they get away with what they're saying. So I submit to you that three-quarters of the people who are writing big books about poetry haven't got any idea of what they're talking about and certainly don't know what they're saying.

NB: And people are very intimidated by it.

MB: Yeah. Now in the academy, what you have is people who are older than Auden was when he had a collection of hats and would ride the buses putting on different hats and trying out different opinions out loud to see what people would say. These are people who ought to have passed that stage, but they will still try out anything, and in the interest of discursive investigation that's fine, but students believe it. Students believe it. And I remember when Timothy Leary dropped in on Iowa City one time, not here for any official reason, but just passing through way back when, and a great crowd gathered at his feet in the house where he was staying and he began to explain all the wonders of drugs. And the best moment occurred when a black student stood up and objected and said,

"What are you talking about? I come from a place where drugs ruin people's lives. That's the real drug scene. You don't know what you're talking about." And, indeed, Leary didn't know what he was talking about. I think language has to be suspected all the time because it's partial, and because it's vague and because it is language. And I think that the best poets listen to themselves. The best poets always write poems which show visibly that they're listening to themselves and responding to what they're saying and questioning themselves as they go on. They must listen to themselves. Otherwise it's just random chords; slower than automatic writing, but not worth much more.

NB: In one of my interviews somebody said that there is absolutely no connection between talent and character.

MB: Ah, that's true.

NB: It seems to me that you've implied that in order to be a poet you have to have a lot of character.

MB: "Character" is a hard term to get a handle on. It gets caught up in moral and, consequently, political considerations and no one really knows what it is, but we can see sometimes in poems how character determines the handling of subject matter. The late James Wright had more character in his poems than perhaps anyone in the sense that he made decisions that came out of character. He wrote a poem called "To the Muse," for example, in which he talks to a childhood friend named Jenny who drowned. At the beginning of the poem he sort of brings her back to life and has her come up and stand on the shore with him out of the suckhole where she drowned and he says, "Well, I know three lady doctors in Wheeling, West Virginia. They keep their offices open all night; I don't have to call them. They'll always be there." He's going to take her to one of the doctors and the doctor will put a tube in and drain the lung. Now I'm just saying this in this awful prosy way, but in the poetry it's pretty wonderful. And he talks about what will happen when the tube is put in: she has to walk around on tip toes and she can't jiggle the needle and stab her heart and so forth. Any young poet could probably write a poem in which he brought somebody who's dead back to life, but then Wright does something that is much more mature and it seems to me comes essentially out of character: he puts her back in the suckhole and he says, "I wish to God I had made this world, this scurvy and disastrous place." He says, "I didn't, I can't bear it either, I know the place where you lie." And he puts her back down in the river because finally he's not God, he's not the agent of creation and he ends up saying, "Come up to me, love, out of the river, or I will come down to you." That to me is an accomplished moment in the poem. Accomplishments that one can talk about in classrooms such as accomplishments of imagery, accomplishments of line and phrasing and rhythm and sound, accomplishments of writing that is, beside all those other accomplishments is this really great accomplishment which one might argue comes out of character which is the decision to be intelligent, to realize that you're not the agent of life and death and that you can't just bring her back to life. Intelligence applied to what the poem is about—that, to me, is worthy and important; poems without intelligence don't interest me at all. Poetry which is just a theme and doesn't have any mentality operating in it interests me less than poetry which makes a turn, or discovery or further exploration in the course of itself. That's along the lines of what I meant by "visible indications of intelligence" in a poem.

NB: You've said about John Logan and Donald Justice that "teaching as well as they have may have cost them something, but it may also have kept them honest."

MB: Oh yeah. Oh yeah! Good! It's awfully hard to bullshit your students if your students are any good. So it makes you keep thinking. I change my mind all the time. I hope I don't so much change my mind as I go further in my thinking, but I'm sure I also change my mind and also sure I contradict myself. As you may know, every book of my poetry is different in certain clear ways. Now I hope it's not just change but growth; but that's for others to decide. My ideas about poetry now are very different, not contradictory necessarily, in relation to what I used to think, but very different. I always told my students that I thought I would be a beginner until about the age of forty. Well, I published *Stars Which See, Stars Which Do Not See* when I was forty and for me, that was sort of the end of an apprenticeship, not because I had planned it but because it just did happen to work out that way. And now I have a pretty good sense of what I want to do. I had to more or less shut up, at least publicly, for two years. I had long periods of silence, and I threw a lot away. I knew what I was reaching for, somewhat, dot, dot, dot.

NB: You said in The American Poetry Review *that a couple of times you'd gone off to places to write and . . .*

MB: Not written. *(Laughter.)*

NB: Could it be that your teaching feeds your writing?

MB: I think that going to work every day helps. Teaching in particular may help because it gets the words stirred up in your mind. You have to use those words, you have to respond to other people's words, so it gets going exactly what one wants to get going in order to write. I myself find having a certain job to do, having a routine to do which isn't overwhelming, is probably better than having nothing to do. I say that with some hesitancy because I hope the university will still occasionally give me nothing to do and I will make up the replacement tasks myself. I've found that the more I do the more I do. Partly I'm that way in general, and partly I tend to write in spurts. This may be just a result of moods, who knows? It may be a result of seasons. We're talking today and it's fall and I love the fall. In the fall, I write poems. I do think that I've cut down on the waste and that I can write more poems, but I think that if that's true for me, it's true because of what I call that apprenticeship until about the age of forty. And I now have a good sense of what it is I want to do and I have a way of doing it no matter what words the poem begins with. That remains to be proved, but I feel that that's true. Rilke worked for Rodin for awhile and therefore, he wrote some essays about Rodin's sculpture. He thought Rodin was a great artist, which he was, and I was struck by the way in which he argued for the excellence of Rodin in one essay where what he really leads up to saying is that Rodin had become so engaged with his art and the world, putting those two into some inextricable relationship, that was not only inextricable but continuous and pervasive, he had become so engaged that he could do no wrong. Those are Rilke's words, translated, "He could do no wrong." And that's a condition I think much to be desired.

NB: He had worked out some kind of . . .

MB: When he worked with stone, when he worked with his sculpture, it would be art. That's all there is to it. I think there are a few poets in this country who have attained that level of engagement with both the materials of their art and the world as they live in it as artists. James Wright had attained it before he died recently. I think that William Stafford is a poet whose every piece of writing is poetry; whether it's good or bad, it's poetry. Whereas when the rest of us write bad poems, they're not even poems.

NB:　I notice that you think your later poems are more accessible.

MB:　Oh, they certainly are. You can't know *how* much more accessible because I didn't publish the first two hundred poems I wrote. I was at one time a graduate student bum with a lot of other graduate student bums here at the Workshop. At the time, I wrote poetry which was absolutely obscure. I can remember Denise Levertov coming to class one time and I had a poem on the worksheet called "Acquaintance/It Happens/Making It Happen" and it was sort of vague and sexual, but it was certainly obscure. There was a line in it that said, "It's as obscure as hell," and she read that line aloud and said, "That's exactly the way I feel about it." At which point, my generous fellow students tried to explain the poem to her and probably to me and to defend it. But the truth is that I was writing very obscurely. There are two things that occur to me right now. One is that obscurity is a kind of psychological defense because when a person can't understand you, you're safe from their reactions. Obscurity is in other cases a way of parading one's abilities. I don't think I meant it that way, at least I hope not. I do think it might have been a defense and I did overcome that. The other thing is that young writers, young people in general, have to be told they're talented before they ever take a stab as writers. It's so hurtful in a way to put one's poems on worksheets at first and to get genuine responses from people who are paying close attention, no matter how kind their responses are, no matter how circuitous they may be; one is so vulnerable. And so you have to have a certain confidence behind that; it may be propped up artificially. A person can be essentially humble and yet he or she can seem very immodest in workshop situations, but I think if one doesn't realize at an early age how unimportant an individual can be one certainly finds out. On the other hand, there's a kind of modesty of style that sometimes goes hand in hand with philosophic modesty that is not necessarily good for the poet. For some poets it's the best they can do; but there's a tendency I think among what we might call workshop writers, if there is such a thing as a workshop writer, to adopt a position with regard to style that is not only central but overly immodest. Neruda, for example, it seems to me, is a man of essential modesty, or his poetry, you could say, is the poetry of a man of essential modesty in the way he thinks about himself, but of great, wonderful immodesty in his use of language, particularly imagery.

NB: I didn't get hold of Stars Which See, Stars Which Do Not See *until I came here and then I read through the first few poems and didn't understand them, but when I went back and reread them, they all seemed very clear. I've never had that kind of experience with poems before.*

MB: I would guess that it's just because the first time reading through, the other person's mind, if it's somewhat eccentric, you don't know what direction it's going, so each time you're yanked along. After you've read it once, you have a sense of where it's going. I'm just guessing. There were two full-length books in between *A Probable Volume of Dreams* and *Stars Which See, Stars Which Do Not See*. As I said before, they were different from one another. The one that followed *A Probable Volume of Dreams* is called *The Escape into You,* a book-length sequence. Some of those poems are difficult; but they're very intense, almost tortured sometimes. It's a very different thing from the book that preceded it. And indeed the book that follows it, *Residue of Song,* is, as the title might suggest, almost antipoetic. It's full of stuff that is aggressively anti-poetic in life, including a poem called "Shit."

NB: I was going to read all of it, but when I started reading Stars *I just kept reading that over and over again.*

MB: Did you get all the way through?

NB: Oh sure, a couple of times.

MB: Good. I'm glad. I like that book. It's not that I don't like all my books, and I do even read them sometimes, but if I had to, I would be happy to have that book represent the way I wrote at one point for a long time. I like it. It feels good somehow. *(Laughter.)* But now I have a new book ready; but it won't come out until next September, probably because I messed around with it for so long.

NB: You've mentioned that your notion of poetry has changed. How?

MB: It's hard for me to say just how my notion of poetry has changed, partly because it's difficult for me to pin down, partly because it's still developing, partly because I don't want to preempt the poems that will occur by talking about it; but I'm willing to try to the extent that I know. I think one learns to write interestingly, if not well, by abandoning oneself to the materials, the actual materials of language. One discovers content. Like the little old lady who's supposed to have gone up to E. M. Forster at a writers' conference and said, "How do I know what I think till I see what I say?" That's the way poetry works. One didn't know one knew such things. And I do think that's the way young poets should go about it, that they should love language more than they love ideas at the moment that they're writing poetry, because ideas are not only valuable for what they are, they're preemptive in terms of other possibilities. So a kind of exploration and abandonment to the materials is really helpful. I've always felt that. When I was working with clay or with photographic plates and chemicals or cornet, I always wanted to do what the medium could do. I wanted to play in the way the cornet could play; well, that was easy to do because the cornet is a singular instrument. I wanted to use the materials of the clay in making pots and, of course, any potter does really use the inherent qualities of the clay and bring them to the forefront. There's another way which I think is perhaps more appropriate, perhaps only possible to an older person who has written for awhile, somebody who has reached middle age, at least, and that is to somehow come at the poem from an area that is prior to language and has to do with imagination and emotion and perhaps the visualization of what it is one is remembering or actually seeing or predicting. It's almost as if the seesaw was formerly slightly down on the form side and on the side of materials as opposed to subject or content, and then it's either more balanced or even slightly down on the side of content. Now this is a dangerous distinction to make because form and content are inextricable even in bad writing and in good writing the inextricability becomes part of the substance. It creates substance, creates content. It articulates things which couldn't be articulated otherwise.

NB: I'm thinking all the time about the difference between writing poetry and doing academic writing. I've come to think that academics tend to shut off their feelings, or are people who shut off their feelings at an early age.

MB: That's right.

NB: They get down to their feelings in convoluted ways. For instance, I'm sure that my obsessions are embodied in the people whom I choose to write about.

MB: Right. Academic writing is more of a process of exclusion. The "problem" is probably the right word for the kind of writing one does for the *PMLA* or *Notes and Queries* or *Philological Quarterly* or whatever, or even for the *New York Review of Books,* God help us, or *The New York Times Book Review,* God help us. It is writing in which an elephant can't appear suddenly. But in a poem, an elephant can appear anytime one chooses and one can use the elephant. There's a great deal of preemptive activity that goes on in writing criticism and reviews. There's a lot that is preempted, whereas in writing poetry, I think, one accepts and accepts and accepts as much as possible and then tries to make use of it. And for me the process of revising a poem, except for matters of clarity, has become the process of accepting what's there and learning how to make it all of a piece. And that's one of the difficulties in teaching a writing workshop. It's so much easier to cut a poem down and make it smaller, but better, than it is to see what it was trying to be that was bigger, which can't be achieved by anything that we do in class, but which should be kept in mind if the poet is ever going to amount to anything bigger.

The poet is really giving himself or herself over to the process and then counting on recognizing and working with what emerges during the poem, but even more so, in my case at least, afterwards. So revision is partly a question of recognition of what's there. That makes perfect sense to me because of all those years I put in as what used to be called a "creative photographer." One of the things one does is to snap the shutter and then go study the negative in a dark room. And there are great photographers who have insisted that the only true way to be a photographer is to previsualize everything, to see it in a ground glass perfectly and then to print the entire negative just as you photographed it. And indeed, I respect that view and often did it that way. But there is another way, and that is to have an intuitive sense of things which carries one into the photographic subject matter and then to work in the dark room to see what it is one has.

NB: And poets are more like that.

MB: Poets do that. That's what they do. Not all of them; there are some people who are very formal and very organized and who succeed in writing wonderful poems this way. But even they are more engaged with the process of their writing poetry than one would normally be in writing essays.

NB: Is it easier for you to write essays than poems?

M: Well, I used to write reviews years ago that were described to me by a friend as very Johnsonian and I did labor over them. Then I quit reviewing deliberately. In fact, I reneged on several commitments. And then I was convinced to write again, and I began to write that series of essays in the *American Poetry Review* and other things, and I decided that I would pretty much write essays when called upon. Whatever the subject given to me was, that's what I would start from. In a sense, it would be very much like writing poems; I would let myself go forward in a conversational way, letting whatever came to mind come to mind, and trying to make a whole out of it. So, I write very informal prose and as I warned a couple of people who've asked me to propose them books, if I put a whole book's worth of it together, I'll probably transcend informality and approach inelegance. But that's the way I want to write. I don't want to give my time over to writing a more structured, elegant, formal, intricate prose. I think there's a lot going on, because of the style I'm writing in, that wouldn't go on otherwise. That's my hope. And it's much more fun this way. It is like once again abandoning oneself to the process.

KELLY CHERRY

NB: A number of the women I've talked to have commented that it's hard for women to take themselves seriously as writers.

KC: There is some truth to that. I was early to start writing, late to start taking myself seriously as a professional. When I was young, I ran into a lot of people who said, "This is just a stage you're going through. All women with dark hair and dark eyes who are eighteen years old think they're going to be poets." One man generously wrote, "I must admit you *do* have a flair, *f-l-a-r-e,* for words." I did waste a lot of time trying to learn to take myself seriously as a professional, but *not* how to take my ambition seriously. I had always done that. I grew up in that kind of family. But taking seriously the act of completing a manuscript, sending it off, recognizing that one rejection didn't mean you were supposed to jump off a bridge but simply meant you were supposed to put it on your file card and send it out somewhere else—all that took time for me to learn.

Also I had a very bad marriage that interfered quite concretely with my writing. I had a very authoritative husband, and as a result, I had been seeing various psychiatrists, most of them ones my husband sent me to, and they would tell me things like, "Because of the double transference process that a girl-child has to go through, she has used up her energy . . ."

NB: They said you couldn't write?

KC: That's right. One of the men recommended an intellectual hobby. He thought archaeology would be a good subject. That I had no interest whatsoever in going out and digging up some old vases

18

was irrelevant. He thought I did need something to occupy my mind, but, of course, women simply don't have the necessary *creative* energy for a subject such as writing. And then, under the assumption that I was learning to be realistic, I kept telling myself that I could not be a writer, I was not a writer, I must learn to rid myself of my "delusions of grandeur," as my ex-husband—he was now "ex"—had called them. I even tried to quit writing permanently; it lasted for about a year.

So there are things like that. I've made those examples particular, but I've seen similar things affect the lives of many women around me. I assume that situation will change. I assume part of what we're doing when we talk about what it's like to be a woman who writes or a writer who happens to be female, is getting these issues out in the open so younger women can be aware of them and not have to go through these hassles. They are foolish problems. I resent that I was stuck with them for awhile and hope that younger women won't have to waste their energy dealing with them, so I think they are a real subject for discussion. It's not a subject I sit around thinking about much because if I were to do that I would be taking away from the time I'd rather spend now on writing. And once I did learn how things worked, I just sat down and started writing like hell.

I think there's something which is even more inhibiting: it's harder as a woman to get published. In 1975 I heard a very intelligent, very good, very nice reviewer for a major magazine say that sometimes they simply can't review a book they like because it's a book by a woman and they've already done two books by women that month. I said, "Did you ever get a book by a man and say, 'Gee, this is nice; but we can't do it because we're already done two books by men this month'?" He was embarrassed. He realized immediately that he had made a *faux pas,* and yet, it was more than a *faux pas:* it was a statement of policy. It is still true that fewer women get published, fewer women are presented in anthologies, fewer women are taught in universities and those things have a very real adverse effect on any woman's career. The only answer is to ignore it and keep on writing and hope that the situation changes or that you break through that barrier. But that barrier is there.

And then women get reviewed differently, even by other women. The reviewers want works that present role models and give the reader some—quote, unquote—insight to take away with them. I am not concerned with the creation of role models. I am not purveying insights; that's the last thing I want to do: every time I've got a character giving an insight, I try very hard to undercut that insight with an opposite insight either from another character or by the book's structure because, unrecognized by the character, the structure of the book is doing something else. I'm making objects. I'm not selling tiny nuggets of wisdom. And yet it's the little nuggets of wisdom that are valued by the reviewers, especially by the reviewers of women's books, whether those reviewers are women or men.

NB: In a review of Fred Chappell's Midquest, *you write, "A woman who commences a voyage of curiosity into the world is doing something riskier than a man who sets sail under the same flag."*

KC: A woman who truly, as I said there, "commences a voyage of curiosity," has no guarantee that there's a home waiting for her when she returns. Virginia Woolf had some sort of guarantee, a couple of contemporary women writers have that kind of guarantee, but I don't have it and, historically, most writers who are women have not had it. Formally, all women lack it; there are not the same literary precedents. Dante is my antecedent, Homer is my antecedent, Joyce is my antecedent, and yet they are not my antecedents in the same direct sense they are for Chappell, just because Chappell is male. When Ulysses is a man, it is guaranteed from the beginning that a woman will remain for him. Penelope is still weaving: she hasn't gone off and had an affair; she hasn't gone back to school to get her B.A. in Education. There's a guaranteed happy ending for the male writer. It's built in from the beginning that wherever he goes, however long it takes him to get there, no matter how many monsters he has to ward off, no matter how messy things are when he gets back, what he has done is important because it has taken him where it was necessary to go in order to reach the ending that was guaranteed at the beginning: an ending of harmony.

The Ulysses who is a woman has no such guarantee. She can set out on that voyage and she may *never* get home again; she can come home, and there's no husband waiting for her because there was none when she left, or he's run off with a younger woman. This is all metaphor, but in reality they do tend to run off with younger women. *(Laughter.)* But using this as a metaphor for formal considerations, it means that the woman who commences this voyage of curiosity has no built-in guarantee that where she is headed is a place where celebration is possible. She may arrive at an ending that is tragic and this may appear to undermine the entire journey.

When Ulysses is a woman, interesting things happen to the story: it is no longer an epic celebration; it can no longer be a comic celebration; it becomes tragic. This does certain things to the language: it's not full of rhetorical or idiomatic devices; it becomes leaner. She may find that structurally she's in a peculiar place because she's got no way to make a conventional resolution, a coordination of vectors in a direction, happy or otherwise. I suppose if I were someday to talk about the difference between writers who are women and writers who are men, my talk would revolve around the question of safety and bravery. The writer who is a woman may get to the end of the journey and find this happy ending, but she doesn't set out with that guarantee. That's where the real anxiety comes in; that's where the real danger comes.

NB: A number of the women writer-teachers I've talked with have said that they get so involved in their students that they can't do their own work while they're teaching. Is that a problem for you?

KC: Well, the way I teach makes a time problem for me. I know from having looked at student papers that other teachers have marked up that this way of teaching is not peculiar to women; it's peculiar to me. *(Laughter.)* I believe in a certain approach that eats up all my time, but my students learn.

I emphasize structure. No student is going to begin to get any portable handle on his work that he can take with him after the class ends unless he gets a solid grounding in structure. The other day a student came to me; she'd had lots of writing classes and still felt she had writing problems that were not being solved and I said, "You know about the little triangle for the short story, don't you?" She said, "The triangle?" And I said, "Well, let's draw a little triangle." As she left she said, "In forty-five minutes I've learned more than I've learned in the past three years." She wasn't flattering me. She had this look—the combination of befuddlement and pleasure and resentment—that revealed plainly she realized she'd been in some sense cheated.

I've never encountered a textbook that properly lays out the structure of the short story so that an epiphany can be technically determined. An epiphany is nothing but a resolution that has been swung to coincide with the climax. Climaxes can be heightened or muted according to whether you lengthen or shorten the moment of crisis that precedes them. Books on creative writing essentially omit paragraphing and omit, for example, the fact that paragraphing is a crucial device for heightening drama. Nobody talks about these things.

If a student learns these things, he can immediately begin to make huge jumps because he has a way of analyzing his own material. This does not mean, and I don't suggest to any student, that a writer sits down and begins by filling in a triangle. You don't. You write out of whatever it is that you're writing out of. But when you do go through all your initial drafts and let them sit for awhile and come back to this stage of revision—at that point, it's *extremely* useful to have these structural things in mind and to be able to think about your story or your poem or your essay or your novel in those terms. You see things that you can do that you had not recognized before.

It seems to me crucial to stress structure. It is crucial to stress the process of draft, critique, revision. If you get the stages mixed up and you do close revision while you're working in the draft stage, you are inhibiting yourself and you will never run into the surprises that you would run into otherwise. People who run into writer's block very often have confused two stages of the process. On the other hand, if you treat revision as if it were a draft stage, you're not going to do the necessary close editing. A certain *slant* on your material, a certain view of your material is appropriate to each stage.

There is one and only one way students can learn revision—and this is where the teacher ends up sacrificing a great deal of his time —and that is by the teacher's doing extremely close editing of at least one or two stories. That takes an enormous amount of time because you cannot do adequate editing of that sort faster than six to ten pages an hour. When I've got two prose classes in a semester, for example, not counting my directed thesis students, I'm reading three or four thousand pages a semester. It gets to be a huge problem.

On the other hand, I'm able to say to my students that I can take any one of them and if he or she will do what I tell him to do, he will have made a quantum leap at the end of the semester. I tell them this does not mean that any of them are going to be Hemingway, say, because they're not starting close enough to that finishing line; but wherever they're starting from, they can take gigantic leaps. This is not all in my head. First of all, I get feedback from the students. After the initial moaning and groaning—they have to do a lot of writing —when they begin to see what they can accomplish, they get excited about it. Another way I know that this method works is that I've had occasion to show a story by X to various teachers who have had X in previous classes and the teachers will say, "My God, what has happened?"

I believe that both talent and genius can be taught. They are taught generally by the self to the self, but it seems perfectly possible to extract and analyze that process and transfer it to a pedagogical situation where the teaching is being done between the selves—a teacher self and a student self. So when people ask the infamous question, "Can writing be taught?" and then answer themselves, "Well, of course, certain devices can, but talent can't." I've learned to smile and say, "Sure." But it's not what I really believe. I believe that talent and genius can be taught—and I don't think genius is simply more talent. I think they are two different things.

Talent has to do with learning what the creative process is, and this takes us back to the business of draft, critique and revision. Once a student grasps that process, he can incorporate it. That's all talent is—learning to have the courage to do something. And you have to learn to have courage. Learning how to have the courage to do something; learning how to see your failures; learning how to tolerate those failures long enough to *do* them and then learning how to tolerate them for an even longer period of time so that you can correct them: this is a process that one can teach oneself, but there's no reason that X cannot teach it to Y.

Beyond that, genius is a state one reaches when one comes to understand the nature of one's understanding. That is to say, talent is the understanding of the creative process, whether we apply it to writing, as we're doing now, or whether we apply it to mathematics, because, after all, creative mathematical or scientific reasoning is not different from creative artistic reasoning; it becomes different in certain of its applications and in certain of its devices and in certain of its other details, but the process is the same. Genius is comprehending not only that process, but also the relation one's own mind bears to that process. Once you learn this and then go on to study and learn the nature of your understanding, the way *your mind* works, you can analyze the way your mind works in relation to that process, and you begin to work with yourself rather than against yourself.

Most of us work against ourselves. Most of us are trying to deal with problems the way they have been dealt with in the past whether or not that approach is congenial to the way our minds work. You could get quite specific about this in terms of how to write an opening for a story, or in terms of what kind of book you're going to write; or you could get sociological about it and talk about the ways women have been taught not to perceive the individual differences between their intelligences. Woman X is not like Woman Y is not like Woman Z and yet we're taught that because we're women, we think in a certain way. So long as you are concerned primarily with the way you as a woman think differently than or like men, you're not perceiving the way in which *your* mind thinks differently from any other mind in the entire universe that has ever or does now exist. And that's what's important to the writer—*your mind.* You have to learn your own mind. When we learn how our mind works, we begin to work with ourselves.

You can teach students this. Almost none of them are going to become geniuses. This is not because genius cannot be taught. It is because it is very *hard work* to become a genius and most people do not want to be geniuses. Most people don't want to make the necessary sacrifices and go through the necessary pain for a dead end. No one can necessarily say they should be doing that. *(Laughter.)* There are all kinds of things in the world and the other things may be much more important. But if X *wants* to do this, X can do this. It hasn't got *zilch* to do with IQ; it hasn't got *zilch* to with some mysterious ability or inability; it hasn't got *zilch* to do with the right hemisphere or left hemisphere. It has to do with an ability to observe one's abilities and lack of abilities.

To bring this back to the classroom, it means that the teacher has a real obligation to recognize that it is not determined from the outset who has—quote and unquote—talent and who does not. If you put in the *right* kind of effort, you will find again and again and again that students you thought did not have—quote and unquote—talent are, at the end of the semester, writing *marvelous* stuff. This approach, on the one hand, heightens the teacher's responsibility to the students, and, on the other hand, liberates the student to some extent from the teacher's control. Every student has the same crack at the goal and the teacher is obliged to become aware of that. The teacher can't say, "Well, X student deserves more of my time than Y student does because X has more talent." If you recognize that given the right materials Y can do what X is doing, then you are obliged to give those materials to both. And then either X or Y or both will go on to use those materials depending on any number of factors—characterological factors, luck . . . all kinds of crazy things no one can predict. But pedagogically you have to allow the possibility of all the students becoming Hemingway.

NB: Do you teach the class like a workshop? Everyone sits around with copies of each other's work?

KC: That's right.

NB: And they still learn to do structural analysis?

KC: Yeah. I bring it out of the students' own work and then every so often I go to the blackboard and get abstract, but I don't go in and say, "We will have a lecture on such and such today." I will pick the material we're going to go over in class according to the particular kinds of problems it's going to present and according to when I want to bring those problems up, so the students stumble on those problems in the course of talking about the material.

I've been all excited about my literary nonfiction class yesterday because it was an excellent session; everyone got all heated. Structural distinctions among forms have been a concern of mine for a long time, and now I'm working up this literary theory book, and these questions come up in a nonfiction class: when am I writing nonfiction and when am I writing fiction? We had a whole hour and a half of abstract discussion with me on the blackboard with "Fiction" on one side, and "Nonfiction" on the other, talking about points of difference. Under such circumstances, everybody is thinking as precisely as you would be in a literature class or in a philosophy class or even a mathematics class.

I knew I was going to give my lecture; I was waiting for the right moment. We got into it because a student had written a very fine essay, but he had at one point given us a description of how a man whose legs had been amputated trained himself on his bars, learning to use his hands and arms in the hospital, and then tacked on the phrase "like a freakish acrobat." We were examining the word "freakish" in that case. All of a sudden, everybody got excited because it threw us into problems of voice, questions of who is the authority in the essay, what does authority mean in an essay, how does the I-persona in an essay differ from the I-persona in a first person short story. Then I knew it was the right moment for me to go to the blackboard and do this number I'd been waiting to do, but I waited until I knew we had something that was going to throw us into it, and then in talking about all this material, I kept bringing it back to specific problems.

In addition to the assigned exercises and the regular material, I have the fiction and nonfiction classes write critiques of one another's major work. Without realizing it, they're doing a whole lot more work because I read the critiques and mark them up. This also means that they come into those classes having read and thought about the material and we are not spending an hour listening to someone read a story out loud. I think that's a waste of class time. You can learn certain things reading a story out loud; therefore, writers should buy tape recorders or pester their friends. There's not time in a semester to sit and listen to everybody read. With short poetry you can do it and, in fact, in my class short poems are always read twice—once by the author and once by someone else.

I encourage writers to go to other departments and to other fields, to other kinds of subject matters, whenever they can. The writer, first of all, is limiting himself if he studies literature to the exclusion of other fields; secondly, there is something to be said for applying your mind to hard-core work. No matter how tough a literature class is, it does not require the same kind of analytic ability that advanced calculus does. I think writers should take advanced calculus. The great danger in a young writer's concentrating exclusively on academic analysis of literature is that he's then likely to spend a very long time in his own work recycling metaphors, but if he's studying geology or biochemistry or mathematics or philosophy or history or French, he is always learning to use his mind and also building up a store of knowledge that can be plundered for metaphor, structural metaphor as well as stylistic metaphor.

It seems to me very, very important for writers to work at, to study, to learn about precisely those subjects in which they are not going to be the smartest kid in the room. If you do always only those things at which you are already "all good," you're never going to learn anything real. All you'll do is acquire more data. Writers should take advanced calculus, even if they're going to get C's or D's. If they don't want to take advanced calculus, they should take Italian. Anything.

There is great value in doing precisely those things at which one is bad. Doing that takes courage. It takes being able to recognize, "Well, when it comes to such and such, I'm not the smartest kid in the room." That's a hard position to place oneself in. I can already, off in the corner, hear certain writers saying, "Well, it's not possible for me to get in that position because I *am* the smartest kid in the room." But that's not true. There's always something at which we are stupid and it's precisely those things we ought to go out and learn about. Doing that teaches us about our limitations and it teaches us something about the way people who are good at those things approach the world. It's often intelligent to be a D student.

Writers have to read all the stuff that a literature major reads, but they do not need to take it apart the way a literature student takes it apart. In fact, often that's detrimental. They need to be able to take things apart from a writer's point of view and to recognize that when he's *writing,* he's not taking something apart, he's putting something together. That's a different process.

NB: What's the difference between the writer's point of view and the critic's?

KC: For starters, take "point of view." Critics always wind up talking about point of view. Point of view is a very minor problem in a creative writing class. All you have to do is remind the student that if one pair of eyes is being used, you can't jump into another pair of eyes unless you've built preparatory platforms for making that leap. All the rest of it about narrators and hidden narrators is hokum. What I do to get rid of that is point out all these points of view that textbooks omit: there is no reason not to use the omniscient "I"—

all that means is that your narrator is God or some god-like being; I point out the use of the marital "we" and the editorial "we." In other words, that particular critical analysis is a) largely irrelevant and b) inhibiting. All that talk about point of view puts blinders on the writer. If the writer just recognizes that any pair of eyes he can imagine is available to him, his problem becomes a technical problem of keeping consistency and of knowing how to make certain transitions.

Critics think writing goes from one to two to three to four to five. They're dealing with the finished work, and if it's been well-written, there is a kind of inevitability about the ending that fools everyone into thinking that it is indeed inevitable. The writer is up here with starting point "one," recognizing there's an infinite number of choices and that because it's Monday or because it's Tuesday, he chooses "two," and then "one" and "two" together narrow that infinity. So there's an infinity that's slightly smaller for "three." He makes this jaggedy path down and it's a good thing he does too; otherwise, there would be a limited number of works that could be written. Because you can go any way you want, every story can be different. The writer is highly conscious of this tricky way of getting through to the end of the story and conscious of all kinds of accidents that contribute to his route. The critic comes along and looks at it backwards and sees what appears to be a linear path from end to beginning and then thinks that because there is this appearance of a linear path, the beginning must have been beautifully all set up with every symbol in place. This is not the way it works in practice.

One does not begin writing with a "theme." That is a word that should be immediately erased from everyone's vocabulary. It's a very dangerous word that leads to enormous misreading, a complete lack of understanding of structure or of what writers are doing, and it's very, *very* dangerous when writers are taught that what they are doing is writing about a theme. The theme is what is there after everything has been put together, and the putting-together creates a kind of magnet. It's terrible to begin writing with a theme. You begin writing a novel, for example, most effectively with a question. I tell my students that if they think they are writing about such and such, one of the very first things they must do is change that declarative sentence to an interrogative one. Begin with a question and not with a statement, because it's the question that's going to take you to interesting places and result in the kinds of ambiguity necessary for a work of art. So it's dangerous for young writers to think about the word "theme," and it's very dangerous for critics to keep throwing that word around because then they're reading as if there were something in a piece of writing that *did* lie at the center and that if somehow you could take away all the artichoke leaves, you would have the theme which is the real thing. It's not the real thing. The real thing is the whole damn artichoke.

NB: What about the idea that being part of the academy shelters writers too much?

KC: Anyone who's ever been through a tenure meeting knows that's not true. *(Laughter.)* It doesn't matter where you are, you have to deal with the fact that you're going to lose people you love, you have to deal with the fact that we ourselves age, you have to deal with the money, you have to deal with other people. Even in the academy, you're still breathing. *(Laughter.)*

I spent fifteen years living out of suitcases doing this odd job and that odd job; sometimes I regret very strongly that I didn't spend fifteen years in the academy. I would have better contacts, I think I would have started publishing earlier, and probably enjoyed a lot of life more. God knows, I could have afforded a decent place to live earlier.

At the same time, it was probably useful for my work that I didn't because I was forced to deal with what it's like to be out in left field. If I had been in the academy, I might not have had the courage to go out into left field. I don't think there's anything inherent in the situation that says a writer in the academy cannot go in left field, but it's up to the writer to do it.

A lot of those writers who have let their work be usurped or drained by academia have a kind of success in academic-literary journals. It is a literature that is safe, not only in terms of not saying anything that will offend anyone in the academy, but also safe formally. It's not adventurous structurally or imagistically or any kind of way. I don't mean they should be writing wild-man poems; I'm talking about the hard work of writing a poem that takes on a big subject and tries to deal with it in all its complexity. You can pick up a magazine and there are all these little poems—"little" not in the sense of length, but "little" in the sense of, what do they do to you? By the time you've read the next one, you've forgotten the first one.

Poets *love* to compare themselves with Adam and to say they are doing an Adamic thing. Poets begin to think that a poem must be an act of praising and since naming is praising, acknowledging the existence of thus and such somehow completes what they must do in the act of writing a poem. There is a whole lot more to writing a poem than naming and people did once think otherwise. The medievalists thought a whole lot more went into literary art than simply naming the things of the world or states of experience. Eighteenth-century writers thought more was involved. A real attempt was made to deal with concepts in fictive and poetic forms. Today we rest too easily on the assumption that poetry is nothing more than an act of praise which is accomplished by naming, and therefore, we are far too easily satisfied with what is essentially an imagist poem. We can talk about surrealism, we can talk about the ways imagism has developed; nevertheless, when you get right down to it, if you open the little magazines, what you're finding is an imagist poem. Fifty years after the fact, it's an imagist poem. You can't turn around without bumping into an imagist poem that calls itself something else. I think more goes into an interesting poem than that and I would like to see poets attempt that more.

NB: Is there any connection between being in the academy and writing that kind of poetry?

KC: I'm afraid MFA programs are partly to blame. I like MFA programs; I think they are good both for writers who are going to be writers and writers who may never write another word in their lives. Nevertheless, I take issue with people who insist that the programs pose no dangers to young writers. There is something that can be called an MFA Style. It's taught all over the place; it's made up of a number of canards. You can spot it. The danger is for students to fall into that kind of writing and then publish some of it. They get that positive reinforcement and then they write more of it and the next thing you know, they've got a job teaching it. Then they are obliged to write more of it because they've got to get a book out. It snowballs.

It seems to me important to be honest about this, to say that because certain things are easier to teach than other things, certain things get stressed in these classes and that may change the proper proportions they ought to have in an ideal world, and to let students know that although a teacher may believe MFA Programs are important, the student also needs to be skeptical of everything going on in the classroom. What you are really trying to teach the student is how to teach himself: how to incorporate this process, how to look at his own work, how to look at other people's work. A student who learns that is also learning to distrust everything you are telling him, I hope. If he's learning that, he's got to be in the process of more and more writing the kind of thing that no one else in the entire world can write: his work. We have a lot of magazines that are full of a lot of the kind of thing a lot of people can do. It's not anybody's work; it's what everybody can do in his spare time. Real writing cannot be done in anyone's spare time. It's everyone's life.

NB: Do you think there could be a connection between your interest in structure and your background in philosophy?

KC: Yes, I'm sure; although I think my interest in philosophy is preceded by something else. My parents were string quartet violinists and they concentrated on the late Beethoven quartets—that was their great love. And also out of a kind of obligation to composers, they made a practice, on every concert, of including one very contemporary quartet, often one that had never been played before. You can't play contemporary music without analyzing structure because you're figuring out how it's supposed to be played for the first time; and there is no more complicated, beautiful—I have no words—there are no higher forms of structure than a late Beethoven quartet. The only thing that seems remotely comparable here is certain kinds of very high mathematics and certainly, in any of the art fields, it seems to me the purest examination of structure and the process of thinking that exists. From the day I was born, every day, I heard my folks practicing these things. I'm not a musician. I wanted to be a writer right from the jump. And I was conscious of the philosophy even before I was conscious of the writing; nevertheless, I was always interested in structure, and it wasn't until a few years ago that I did have this realization that I had simply translated my parents' concern to another medium. So I think *that* antedates both the interest in philosophy and writing.

As a writer, I did begin by being interested in structure and that's one reason I was late to develop as a writer although I was writing intensively very early. But someone who is primarily interested in structure and interconnections of ideas is likely to take longer to make a connection with daily texture, and it is the sense of detail that readers respond to first. I'm often amazed by the extraordinary sense of detail that some of my young writers have and I say, "My God, how did you see that? It took me twenty years before I opened my eyes enough to see that." I was looking at the skeleton, not at the flesh. I've had to learn to look at the flesh and I feel that I *have* learned, but this is opposite from the way most writers develop and it is certainly opposite from the way that almost all writers who have early success develop. Any writer who is going to do something serious and lasting has got to have them both, and a lot of other things besides that we haven't mentioned, but I did start from the inside out and you get published from the outside in.

In a way, I think it's advantageous to begin from the inside. If you have early success, it's very hard to get away from what you are being praised for, and to create that ultimate lasting object or series of objects, you have to be able to do both the outside and the inside. The person who is learning structure and moving from the inside out is not having that kind of praise. Of course, he's got another problem: dealing with rejection. But once you reach the point where you are able to do the surface of things and you are then being published, you've already got all that background to work with.

We have this feeling that writers who get attention when they're young may crack up, but if they don't and if they go on to write book number two and three and four and five, they're OK. They may be OK, but the odds are they're rewriting book one and that's every bit as dangerous. And then people who become very famous tend to become personalities rather than persons without realizing it, feeling that they have to write a certain kind of book and package themselves a certain way. I don't think any of that's conscious. That's the great danger for an American writer: we are usurped by the entertainment industry. It does not seem nearly as threatening as the danger faced by those writers who live in countries where their lives, careers, are usurped by the political industry, but it is a very real threat. It's a different kind of jail, often a very comfortable one, but every bit as limiting to the writer's work.

This does not mean I don't want to be famous. I would jump at it, and I would jump at the money even more. I would jump at both —believe me! But I think it's very *real* danger and not only in terms of great fame and great money. This happens in one's tiny circle. You get reviewed by a certain number of little magazines and you begin to be aware of your image in those magazines. Delmore Schwartz had a very rarefied fame; it did its work anyway. So even those of us who have not had best-sellers need to be aware of this problem and need constantly to inspect our work and our characters to do our best *not* to have this sort of thing happen.

NB: I'm surprised that you are planning to do scholarship.

KC: This book is a theoretical book. It's philosophy. It involves scholarship because I have to do a lot of reading, but I'm actually proposing a new poetics. The structural considerations I've been concerned with for many years, both theoretically, because structure is a subject I think about, and practically, because it's a subject I deal with every time I sit down at the typewriter and decide whether I'm writing a poem or a story or what, and also pedagogically, because it comes up again and again in my classes; that interest in structure has coalesced, much to my surprise, with work I was doing when I was a graduate student in philosophy. I have no idea why the two suddenly fused. I had in mind to write a short book about formal variation. I was going to do three informal, personal essays about fiction, nonfiction, and poetry, and all of a sudden this idea went slam up against this other stuff and I was involved in a systematic development of a new poetics.

It is the first attempt to write a comprehensive poetics that takes logically into account the writer's working relation to his material. Many writers have written theoretically, but they have not been philosophically trained and have been unsystematic. Coleridge was splendid, but hardly systematic. And then we've got people like Aristotle, but Aristotle was not scribbling plays on the side. We've never had someone interested in these two things together before, and I am. I've been deeply distressed by what's going on in some contemporary literary theory with structuralists and deconstructionists and the reader response people. All that stuff is philosophically suspect. They pick up Peirce's writing on signs without paying attention to the fact that Peirce predicated those writings on his papers on logic and epistemology. They conduct a wholesale transportation of modern physics into critical theory without first studying physics. I am also distressed by some of those same theorists insofar as they don't understand what a writer is doing when a writer is at a typewriter.

A lot of writers say, "Good God, why are you thinking about this stuff, and anyway, you're being too rigid." I don't think I'm being rigid. I think I'm constructing a system that allows us to read many kinds of literature with a great appreciation of what different forms can do. This kind of analysis extends the writer's awareness of forms and therefore extends the writer's capabilities. Still, a lot of writers *don't like* to think this way. They don't like abstractions. And a lot of philosophers *don't like* . . .

NB: *Big arguments.*

KC: That's right. And a lot of literary critics don't want to think writers have anything to think about literature. So here I am, feeling like an anomaly except that, now that I have managed to make them come together, I have found, much to my *delight,* that *all* these people are suddenly interested. The feedback I've gotten has been wonderful. It confirms my sense that the book is important and makes me feel it is worthwhile for me to sacrifice the time one way or another to write this book.

I not only see no contradiction among the various kinds of writing, but I believe they reflect and refract one another. I often find that working on a poem will, for example, help me to understand some problem that I'm facing with a novel. They may be different forms, but, after all, they're all part of literary art, and the more familiar you are with one facet, the more you are learning, in a backwards sort of way, about another facet, and having learned all that, whether it's intuitive or conscious, it seems a shame not to walk around the diamond and explore that other facet. And so you keep going and there turn out to be more and more facets. I don't see any reason not to do it all and not to give oneself wholly to whatever it is one is doing. It's all words. It's all the same thing and what makes it the same thing is that it's all structurally so various and fascinating.

I certainly hope I get a grant. I need the time. I feel I have paid my dues. I have paid my dues in terms of hanging in there, but I mean quite specifically *technically* I have paid my dues. I know a great deal about structure and technique and I have this *marvelous, exhilarating* feeling of being master of my tools and of having a wide range of tools and now I'm eager to use them. There are all these things to be done and I've earned the right to do them. I want to do everything. That may sound grandiose, but it seems to me an entirely reasonable and intelligent ambition. Anything else is a truncation that ultimately leads to self-frustration and depression. I want to do my damndest to do as much as possible and as many different kinds of things as possible.

SEYMOUR EPSTEIN

NB: I just read an article that began, "Name three good essayists with Ph.D.s," suggesting that there's a conflict between studying literature and making it, and yet a lot of people try to do both. Why?

SE: Graduate schools are not really all that much interested in the creative process. To make an entirely different set of rules for someone who is there because he is creative just defeats them. And I can understand why. Tradition and their set of values is immediately challenged. If the creative person is someone apart, then why look for a degree? Hemingway didn't get a degree. Faulkner didn't get a degree. But Hemingway and Faulkner lived in different times. The student interested in writing these days is rather in the position of the scholar in the dark ages who found sanctuary in the church. Your creative person finds sanctuary in the university today. Making a living as a writer is such a hazardous business that there has to be something to fall back on. What the writer falls back on is teaching. In an unsatisfactory world, it's the best place for the writer to be. Therefore, he is encouraged to do those things which will secure him a job. And then he can continue his writing because everything else aside, nothing offers as much free time to the writer as being a teacher. So for a variety of reasons, the student is encouraged to go through that horrible experience to get a graduate degree and to write at the same time. And it is extremely difficult.

NB: What do you try to teach the students in your fiction-writing classes?

SE: I think that generally you have two approaches to writing fiction: the kind of person who wants to tell a story and a writer who

36

is impelled to write because there is some kind of human quality that is embodied in a person and you want to write about that. I belong to the second category. I tell my students that these are two absolutely legitimate approaches. It doesn't make a difference which end you come from, you're going to have to supply the other. If you're fascinated by human beings, you're going to have to find a story to tell about them. If you're fascinated with a story, sooner or later you have to people that story with credible human beings. If there are no credible human beings, then the whole story weakens and falls apart.

I came to writing because I fell in love with writing. There's that ancient superstition about power being given to man when he finds the right word, gives a name to something. That is the Promethean fire. I felt that way because of the wonderful things that I read. But people today do not read. There's no getting around it. They do not read. They do not want to write because they have fallen in love with words. They want to write because they no longer go to church. And if there isn't a God and if there isn't a big story, they'll have to invent their little one. We've gone on for a long time now with the results of Darwin's inquiries and we're finding into the fifth and sixth generation that it is a lonely place without something that will celebrate our existence. So the individual tries to celebrate his own existence. I think that this is the reason for this great increase in creative writing courses and creative writing programs.

Because they have not read, and because they have not come to writing through that particular process, I think that they are missing the whole regimen of responsibility of the writer. They have not been inculcated with the responsibility of the writer. Even the carelessness of a writer must be deliberate, and he must know what he is doing. To be just generally sloppy makes me feel that even if your ideas are good, I'm not interested because you have somehow breached a contract with me.

What I try to do is inculcate that sense of responsibility. One student turned in a science fiction story and I really laced into him. I said, "I don't particularly care for science fiction; it's not my thing. But if you care for science fiction, then you should have enough respect for what it is you're writing to at least go to the damn library and look up something, look up some of these scientific terms. You talk about a city, a city where there's a million workers in a single complex and you let it go at that. How did it come about? How does something like that come about?" What you try to do is continually increase the parameters of their perception. If they wish to write about science fiction, it is their responsibility to tell me about genesis, and time past, and time future. It is their responsibility to collect a convincingly technological language to talk about it. If you haven't got one, don't write science fiction. And I quote from a friend of mine, Issac Asimov, who said he became a writer not because he wanted to write science fiction, but because he had this enormous scientific background and he got bored with being a microbiologist. And he was also a mathematician. He was coming to it the right way. He had the material. If you go there with two sticks and a band-aid, you're not going to write anything.

NB: What do you do in the classroom to "inculcate that sense of responsibility"?

SE: I have the students write stories. When they come into class they have to reproduce the stories and get enough copies so that everyone in the class has a copy. I will not discuss the story unless it has been read by everybody in the class. When it has been read by everybody in the class, I have a set routine. I will criticize a story and I will underline and I will make marginalia: "This is good," "This is confusing," "Here I have a sense of character," "I don't know what or who you're talking about here." I make general comments throughout the whole story. After finishing reading the story, I will take two loose-leaf papers and type out a general criticism of the story. One copy is going to be attached to the manuscript which is going back to the student; one becomes my permanent record of my comments about the stories. That is the record on which I base the grade and which tells me something about the progress of that person. I tell my students there is one area that is taboo: you do not criticize anyone for the story per se. Any area of experience that anybody wants to write about is perfectly legitimate. It is not a legitimate challenge to say, "Why did you write about that?" You don't question that. If you want to criticize a story, I don't want "This stinks," or "This is a pretty good story." I want specifics. If you think that there was good characterization, I want you to underline the parts of the story where you think it was good. If you think that it falls off in articulation, in coherence, or whatever, I want that underlined too.

Now in teaching a creative writing class, very often I will come across stories which are rather hopeless. There doesn't seem to be any talent. There doesn't seem to be any imagination. There doesn't seem to be any love of words. Then I'll come across a paragraph and that paragraph is like a patch of green in a brown wilderness. Then you grab that student and say, "Why did you write that?", "What happened when you wrote that?" And then you try to bring the person and that internal experience together and try to persuade the person that's what made him write that way. It's no accident. It's because his mind made contact with something that was productive in that kind of writing. When you bring that person in contact with the most fecund part of his mind and experience, that's the most important function you perform.

NB: But I doubt that an undergraduate or even a graduate student could have the kind of insight I see in your work.

SE: Mozart composed an opera at six or seven years of age, a perfectly playable opera. There are mathematical geniuses at the age of eight or nine or ten. There are child prodigies in dancing, in painting, not in writing. You don't have any child prodigies in writing because you cannot have human insight without experience. I don't expect my undergraduates to have the insight I have. They can't. And yet I have gotten stories from students in which there was an astonishing amount of sensitivity to life. I recognize myself in the story. I recognize those moments when you feel like you're up on a mountain pass about 12,000 feet high and it's difficult to take in air. There is that rarefied feeling, that moment when you'll break through the tissue of life and you'll have a revelation about it. So the function of the teacher in a creative writing course is to look for the green patch, to see where it is, and to nourish it and water it and see that it grows.

NB: It sounds like you're a very careful teacher; I have to think you get something from teaching besides sanctuary.

SE: I like people of this age. I have sons about the same age. The energy and the possibility of getting anything done in this hideous world rests with them and passing on whatever you think is good, whatever is useful to them, can be a joy and is certainly a responsibility. I like them. They're unspoiled. Most of them can't write, unfortunately.

ALLEN GINSBERG

NB: *I was confused by the tapes of your classes. Are they literature classes or writing classes?*

AG: I don't make a distinction. Although in writing classes people presumably write poems and bring them in and have them criticized and in literature classes people presumably study other people's texts and don't write, the best teachings I got from Kerouac and Burroughs was hearing them pointing out gems of language and rhythm and perception in world literature as well as in my own which turned me on to say, "I can do that" or "I did that" or "This is just like my brain." So what I'm doing is presenting texts which give the students permission to be as intelligent as they secretly are. So it's a writing class and it's also a literature class, but I don't think the teaching of writing necessarily involves the full-time examination of the students' texts or the teacher's texts. I think it's a byplay of intelligence between the students and the teacher on anything, whether it's Shakespeare or a brick wall. It's indicating to the student how to use perception, not necessarily in written form, in terms of body English: how to sit in a chair, how to be aware of breath, how to walk across the street. Knowing how to walk across a street is the same thing as knowing how to write a haiku; learning how to walk across the street is the same thing as learning how to write *The Brothers Karamazov.*

NB: *"If the mind is shapely, the poem (art) will be shapely."*

AG: Yes. The thing is to get under the students' skin and arouse enough enthusiasm that they get under their own skin. This means

41

allowing yourself to be yourself in class. My own best teachers were William Carlos Williams, William Burroughs, Gary Snyder, Gregory Corso, and Jack Kerouac. I learned by hanging around with them, from watching their reaction to cars going down the street or a story in the newspaper or TV or a movie image or a sunset or moon eclipse; when you see the intelligence of somebody reacting to the phenomenal world, you learn by imitation. You see beauty and you want to share it.

My best learning was just being myself with them and they giving me permission to be myself and then discovering myself with them —how funny I was. So you've got to encourage the student to discover himself and how funny he is and the only way you can do that is by letting yourself be yourself in class which means not teaching, but being there with the students and goofing off with them. The best teaching is done inadvertently.

The oriental theory is such, called "darshan." People will go across India to visit Gandhi or Ramakrishna or Great Lama, to take darshan, which means just to look at them, see how they move their arms, how they carry themselves. It's not a mystical matter; it's seeing and examining someone whose intelligence is unobstructed, whose breath is unobstructed, whose body is unobstructed, whose psycho-physical make-up is unobstructed or full of character. That isn't a rationalistic or mystical or mysterious matter—it's common sense.

You finally have to get down to cases and take a look at what [the students] put down on paper because you could talk beautifully and they could talk back intelligently and sympathetically and full of erotic clarity and you think they understood, but then when they write down something, it might turn out to be the most dreary, third-rate imitation of Rimbaud-Dylan . . . which happened to me the other day. I ran into a student who struck me as radiant and then I read what he wrote—he had only two vivid words out of a page and a half of romantic drivel. So you have to look at the work and see if students are on the level you think they are.

Williams taught me by going over my poetry, *Empty Mirror.* I sent him eighty pages of stuff and he separated forty pages that he thought were really good and he told me what he thought was "inactive" among those forty pages, said I ought to cut it out. I said, "But it's part of the writing, isn't it?" He said, "One active phrase is better than a whole page of inert writing because nobody will ever read or reread it, whereas the active phrase, even if it's not a complete sentence, is more interesting." He put two pages in front of me. One had an active phrase that didn't come to anything as a whole poem, but was fine as a fragment, like a Greek fragment, a piece of Sappho that's still brilliant even though it's only part of a clause versus a whole page of something that's not active. So he said, "Cut down to what's active."

There's another useful principle Mark Van Doren pointed out. He used to write book reviews for *The New York Herald Tribune* and almost every one of the reviews was intelligent and sympathetic; he was always talking about something absolutely marvelous. I said, "What do you do with a book you don't like?" and he said, "Why should I waste my time writing about something I'm not interested in?" So, in looking at students' writing and teaching other poetry, it's a waste of time to try to tell them what they're doing wrong. It is not a waste of time to point out examples of active language to them and give them an arrow in the direction you think they should go. You might briefly give some explanation of what is wrong with a phrase like "a dim land of peace" or "I am suffering the terrible illusion of being born into the mystery of nature." You might try to analyze it, but it's like trying to explain what *isn't* there; so the best thing you can do is point to what *is* there. Use every situation to enlighten in the direction of what is practically apprehensible and useful. Point out that part of their nature that is already successful and apparent and concretized and palpable. Attacking what's impalpable is like attacking the ocean. Same thing in terms of poetry samples. Some teachers used to take great delight in mocking bad poetry; it might be more interesting to constantly uplevel the whole discourse by working with material that's active.

NB: As I understand it, you think that in order to write poetry well, one must let go of pretentions and accept whatever comes up.

AG: Yeah.

NB: That's hard to do.

AG: Then maybe you don't understand what it means because it seems to me easy. What's so hard about it?

NB: Well, you've said that Kerouac had to keep telling you to let go.

AG: Yes.

NB: And that it took you a long time to be able to do it.

AG: Yeah, because I thought I was supposed to do something different than what came naturally. It wasn't that I couldn't get to my nature. It was that I thought my nature was unacceptable for high class poetry. I thought that high class poetry meant something besides just ordinary mind; I thought it meant some other kind of mind than the one we've got. Trying to fake another kind of mind or another kind of language or another kind of perception constantly leads poets into these paradoxical situations where they fake something that might be imitatively interesting, but, on the other hand, ultimately is *uninteresting to them.* They dry up at the age of forty or they have writing blocks because they're not making sense on any level, but they think they're supposed to make sense on some level they can't get to. It's like a Marxist with an idea that his writing is supposed to be social for the people, except he can't think of anything social for the people *(laughter)* and so he stops writing because he never understood what "social for the people" means to begin with. It's such a generalization, it has no real, immediate, practical application. But if someone is dominated by the conditioned reflex in that phrase and criticizes every immediate reaction he has according to this phrase he doesn't understand anyway which is supposed to be an idea . . . . Like, "My ambition as a writer is to be elegant." Who knows what the fuck "elegance" is? Everything you write, nothing is elegant; so you feel that your writing is terrible or you stop writing. So "letting go" meant letting go of an arbitrary idea that didn't make any sense.

NB: Where did you get it?

AG: From the teaching of poetry at Columbia and the community around Columbia.

NB: Well, most of your students have been to school and some people have suggested that schools teach people to lie.

AG: Well, Socrates' school didn't teach people to lie. I don't think Black Mountain taught people to lie. Run-of-the-mill schools do.

Waitress: Coffee?

AG: No thanks.

NB: Yes, please.

AG: Better watch out. You'll get cancer of the pancreas! I don't think the nature of school is to make people lie. I think it's the nature of capitalist supported or communist state supported schools; schools tied up with major exploitative economic and bureaucratic systems naturally are supportive of bureaucracy.

NB: Your students are not five years old; they've been to a lot of schools. So when they hear, "Write down your perceptions as honestly as you can," they have probably learned that they ought to have certain kinds of perceptions.

AG: Oh, so how do you get them to locate their own perceptions rather than imitating mine? How do I get them to write in a style that's different from *Howl?* By demonstrating in the classroom how those perceptions are arrived at by me, by arriving at such perceptions during the course of the conversation in the classroom so that we all arrive at the same perception together or by pointing it out to them when inadvertently they've let loose with a perception that's native to them, by checking out the perceptions of other poets and texts and pointing them out as examples, particularly Charles Reznikoff and Williams because their basic method is "ordinary mind," then check out the student's own writing, then in personal conversation and contact, or by lovemaking with the students in bed when appropriate . . .

NB: Are you serious?

AG: I'm totally serious.

NB: Okay.

AG: I believe the best teaching is done in bed and I am informed that's the classical tradition, that the present prohibitive and unnatural separation between student and teacher may be some 20th century wowser, Moral Majority, un-American obsession. The great example of teaching was Socrates, and if you remember "The Symposium," the teaching method there involved Eros. So Eros is the great condition for teaching. It's healthy and appropriate for the student and teacher to have a love relationship whenever possible.

Obviously the teacher can't have a love relationship with everybody in the class and the student can't have a love relationship with every one of the teachers because this is strictly a human business where some people are attracted to others, but where there is that possibility, I think it should be institutionally encouraged. The immediate question that arises in our environment is the exploitation of the student by the teacher and vice versa, but that problem arises in any love relationship and does not rise any more in the student-teacher relationship than in any other relationship. So it's a fake issue. It's a worry about what people will think rather than a native worry about the actual situation. Of course such a situation depends on the tact and intelligence of the teacher. If you have a gorilla professor or a man-eating Amazon professoress or a completely neurotic person, then the relationship will be neurotic and most relationships are neurotic and that's the way life is. On the other hand, I wouldn't worry about it because that's part of the learning process.

When you read *The New Yorker,* or other accounts of the academic or poetic circuit, it's commonly accepted that it does happen, if not universally, at least more often than not. So what we're discussing is not something specialized to me; we're just opening the discussion of normal, average behavior. We're talking about what goes on rather than what ideally should go on or what a minority of adventurous spirits persist in. The majority of ordinary people behave this way. That such a teaching relationship as an ideal would be considered reprehensible and scandalous, although it's universally practiced in the academy, means there's some basic lie as to educational method that's been universally accepted for conscious talk although the behavior is different. The difference between actual behavior and conscious discussion, where you do one thing and say another, is double bind, and that leads to schizophrenia and alienation and confusion. So the reason most academic and institutional teaching is difficult is because it creates emotional schizophrenia where the impulses and the behavior are in one direction and the speech and instructions are in another. That's a basic stress on both students and teacher: the natural overflow of affections and intelligence and energy are checked.

If you don't acknowledge the actual conditions, you can't, in class, point to ordinary mind, you can't point to epiphany and you can't point to the recognition of one's own nature. So while there is a great blank or amnesia or evasion or suppression or avoidance [of] a major area of emotion and human relationships going on, it makes it more difficult for the poet who is depending on intelligence about human nature for his subject matter. It makes it difficult for the teacher to point to instances present in the classroom and in the community. So it makes teaching almost impossible because one of the bases of poetry is frankness. When there's an obstruction of intelligence in classroom communication because of law or convention, then it's not quite possible to communicate. If you can't communicate, you're not teaching poetry to poets. So that's a fundamental insight to which we should relate.

It doesn't mean you have to make love to your students; it doesn't mean you have to talk about it all the time in class; it just means that the teacher has to consciously relate to that situation in a creative and open way. Even if the relationship is an avoidance of it, it's got to be conscious. If it's subliminal, then the entire nature of intelligence becomes fogged and if you have foggy intelligence, you have imprecise poetry. That's why it's important to discuss it consciously; otherwise, you get platitudes that have no grounding in nature.

Shakespeare, Chaucer, Milton, Blake, Whitman—those poets considered greatest and who are the staple of what is taught would laugh at the manner of teaching and the treatment of Eros in the teaching of their work. So everything has been turned upside down in the regular teaching situation.

The reason I'm going on so is that you seemed surprised when I said the best teaching is done in bed.

NB: At most universities, it's the only thing you can be fired for except gross incompetence.

AG: Yes, of course that's it. It's the one thing you can get fired for. If you look at the great teachers, just in the ordinary academic scene, you'll find all the gossip and scandal and humor of Coyote, the American Indian god, who is a trickster hero and who's beyond the law, but isn't beyond human nature. Is human nature beyond the law? It's not perfectly normal for students and teachers to be afraid of each other erotically. It's just a social convention and if at this point, someone can't tell the difference between a dopey social convention and universal human nature humor, the whole discussion is hopeless—particularly when a poet is teaching and a poet is not supposed to love the girl he teaches or the boy he teaches? Ridiculous. That's absolutely absurd. Throw the homosexual shot in the pot too to make it even more outrageous and you have something totally ancient and classical and at the same time, totally outrageous from the limited middle-class, wowser, boo-boo, bourgeoisie point of view.

So if you open up the notion of teaching to the philosophy of the boudoir, you have a different angle. My own experience is that a certain kind of genius among students is best brought out in bed: things having to do with tolerance, humor, grounding, humanization, recognition of the body, recognition of ordinary mind, recognition of impulse, recognition of diversity. Given some basic honesty, some vulnerability on the part of teacher and student, then trust can arise. Mutually acknowledged vulnerability leads to mutually acknowledged trust—erotic vulnerability, scandal vulnerability, social vulnerability, the fact that raw human nature is vulnerable anyway which is characteristic of great poets like Keats and Hart Crane, that raw open heart that's so useful in poetry. Given a conscious acknowledgement of vulnerability, you have a basis to begin teaching poetry.

NB: Most of the people I've spoken with think it's important to read work out loud and you've explained why that's valuable.

AG: Well, probably I've talked enough about vocalization in other interviews. Just one sentence—poetry and language exist in the dimension of sound as well as ideas and letters, so in order to have unobstructed intelligence, you have to be apprehending and hearing sound.

NB: Some people have run into trouble with colleagues in the English Department.

AG: It's the same thing like you're not supposed to make love. The poets who don't think you're supposed to make love and don't think you're supposed to read verse out loud are also the ones who have a limited idea of what's classic and what's traditional and don't like open form and don't like blues, they only like the closed forms that were practiced one hundred years ago. They only like the dead, closed forms like the sonnet; they don't like the rhymed, triadic, five-foot line exhibited in the blues, which is also a classic form, but they never heard of it as a classic form although it has a name, a nomenclature, and a practice and created what may be the largest and most sophisticated body of literature produced in America:

I'll give you sugar for sugar that you'll get salt for salt
I'll give you sugar for sugar that you'll get salt for salt
Baby, if you don't love me, it's your own damn fault.
Sometimes I think that you're too sweet to die
Sometimes I think that you're too sweet to die
Other times I think you ought to be buried alive.

That's Richard "Rabbit" Brown's "James Alley Blues." So there's this tradition of texts which will be classic in a couple of hundred years but which would be avoided as literature by the same people who don't believe in lovemaking or reading aloud *(laughter)* or talking frankly.

NB: A number of people have said it's important for students to receive exposure to lots of cultures, but that blues is excluded from the academy, American Indian Literature is excluded from the academy, Chicano Literature is excluded from the academy, so there's no American Literature being taught in the academy. It's all derivative European Literature.

AG: Or American high literature like Pound, Williams, Marianne Moore—which is great, but the actual community literature which in ancient times was considered the important thing, the Homeric community literature, is ignored in contemporary letters.

There may be some argument about American Indian Literature because it's a minority literature; Chicano Literature because it's a minority literature; but blues is a majority literature that every white and black person in America knows by heart, has feeling for, listens to and does. Everybody hears blues; everybody sings it; everybody that listens to Dylan, the Rolling Stones, Beatles, all rock and roll, as well as the people who are smart and go to the black originals. So it's a universally practiced form which is ignored as literature. Right there is a case of neurotic amnesia—obliterating this whole area of literary practice as if it did not exist. The reasons for it are complicated. It has to do somewhat with racism, somewhat with rigidity of consciousness, so that spontaneous and oral forms are not brought to the notice of those few students who would pick up on the form—it would alter their perception of the phenomenal world —because the blues are franker about human relations than most literary poetry.

It might be just a class thing, that upper classes, the non-laboring classes, the upper bureaucratic, exploiting classes who live on paperwork but don't do actual physical labor, and whose paperwork exploits the physical work of other people, don't want to know about the physical world. Sound is the physical world, sex is the physical world, Eros is the physical world, spontaneous blues—the existence of a large body of universally practiced poetic forms in the actual physical world—all of these are eliminated and anesthetized. So it may be the practice of an elite group of paper-shuffling bureaucrats who are trying to suppress evidence of the existence of a suffering physical world.

John Crowe Ransom, in one of his greatest poems, addressing the graduating class at Harvard, ended his poem:

And if there's passion enough for half their flame,
Your wisdom has done this, sages of Harvard.

It's a Phi Beta Kappa poem written by the eminent, classical, conservative poet John Crowe Ransom, a most respected New Critic in America. Even he criticized the education at Harvard for having dampened the physical passion of his students. So this is no bohemian insight that we're arriving at; this is old granny wisdom, even in the academy. It was a complaint that William James took up when he was there. That was the cause of the whole pragmatic philosophy—checking out what was actually happening instead of stories about it. Check out the physical body. It would even apply to religious experience, that you have to examine the specimens, the visionary experience, rather than make generalizations deductively.

NB: And you certainly know about all kinds of literature, not only the blues.

AG: The idea that recognition of the body, recognition of Eros, and recognition of sound would exclude rational intelligence is an error of judgement that only someone locked into rational intelligence and nothing else, neither imagination nor body nor feeling, would make. That's Blake's classical division; there are four Zoas, four basic principles of human nature: there's reason, there's feeling, there's imagination, and there's the body. If reason dominates the body and imagination and the heart, it becomes a tyrant and winds up a bearded old man inside the cave of his own skull tangled up in the knots of his rationalizations. If the heart tries to take over and push too far, then it becomes a parody of sentimental gush. If the imagination tries to take over and exclude reason and balance and proportion and body, you get some nutty LSD head, jumping naked in front of a car saying, "Stop the machinery!" and getting run over. The body trying to take over, you get some muscle-bound jock. So you have to have them all in balance. To have them all in balance would mean that reason would have its part to play as "sweet science." There's a line in Blake's *Milton* about reason as "sweet science" rather than "horrific tyrant." Reason has become a "horrific tyrant" in Western Civilization and created the nuclear bomb which can destroy body, feeling, and imagination. So there's no sacrifice of intellectual labor in acknowledging the existence of other modes of intelligence, as in body, feeling, and imagination.

The difficulty with Urizenic thought is that it bounds the horizon —"Urizen," Horizon. It makes a boundary so you don't see beyond the limits of conceptual thinking. So you don't hear the *sound* of poetry, you don't feel the rhythm of poetry, perhaps you don't even imagine the vast implications of the poem; but you get pedantically hung up on some rearrangement of mental forms in the poem. The poem finally presents manners rather than the entire gamut of human feeling and intelligence and rhythm and prophecy.

You remember Socrates was given the hemlock for corrupting the young and Socrates was *certainly* a great educator; he was the acme of the teacher, both of philosophy and poetry. Socrates slept with his students, corrupted the young, was kicked off the campus, was driven out of society and made to take hemlock. Christ, the greatest teacher of all, was taken by the forces of law and order and crucified. Buddha was relatively successful, lived to a ripe old age; however, because he was a very great teacher, he had to deal with ignorance and there are some forms of ignorance that are pretty implacable, like the ignorance of the guy who killed John Lennon, Mark Chapman—who was attracted by Lennon's light, but also confused by the light and so struck out murderously, aggressively with his innocent stupidity. So old Buddha was given bad pork to eat by a jealous cousin. Buddha did quite well, but there still is a certain recurrent unreasonable ignorance in mankind which might be resolved after a long, long time; but confusion has its crises and its aggressions and there's no insurance against it. Actual teaching in the most traditional forms has led to conflict with ignorance in which ignorance has taken violent action, so it should be kept in mind that though true teaching won't necessarily provoke a vicious counter-reaction, when somebody gets into trouble, it may be that they are teaching well. Every scandalous teaching should be examined with that in mind as the background: that the classical teachers were scandalous or were perceived to be scandalous by those who didn't understand their teaching; the ignorant thought it was something extravagant rather than something obvious.

CLARENCE MAJOR

NB: You make a number of statements that seem to link finding yourself as a writer with finding yourself as a person. Do you believe that the two are connected?

CM: Yeah, I think the two processes are integral and interchangeable and inseparable—the continual redefinition of self and the process of learning how to write every day. I find that it's an endless lesson; you don't really carry that much information and skill from one piece to the next unless you're doing the same thing over and over. Each act of writing becomes a whole new experience which is why it's so difficult. It's not like a nine to five job where you know what you're supposed to do every day, so I think, yeah, I think the self is involved in that process. You're different every day and if you're trying to do something that's worthwhile, then you're going to have to rediscover yourself, and rediscover a new approach, a new technique, a new way of getting at the same old things about life.

NB: So every day when you sit down and write, you have to reconnect with yourself?

CM: Yeah, I think so. I think a lot of that happens automatically and unconsciously. I don't think we deliberately go about it in a programmed way; I think it's just there as an instinctive demand on the self.

NB: You wrote, "It was finally through the hard work I put into All-Night Visitors *that I came (in Ralph Ellison's words) 'to possess and express' the spirit and understand* with feeling *the footnotes on who and what I was."*

CM: Umm, yeah.

NB: Is there any connection between that discovery and the fact that you were able to write your next book, NO, *so quickly?*

CM: I really didn't know how to write a novel when I wrote *All-Night Visitors;* I took the best parts of three novels that didn't work and somehow pulled them together and created this novel called *All-Night Visitors.* But I never had any sense of direction while I was writing that book; I had to discover it as I worked on the book and finally I saw how I could pull it all together. That's when I sat down and wrote the book.

NB: Do you feel that once that focus was established, it carried over to your later work?

CM: Well, with *NO* it was different because I had a concept; I had a vision of that novel. I knew what I wanted it to be and it came pretty close to being what I wanted it to be. So I wrote it on an endless sheet of paper, which made it a lot easier. The things that I learned writing *All-Night Visitors* really didn't carry over to *NO.* And I wasn't able to use anything that I learned from writing *NO* in the process of writing *Reflex and Bone Structure.*

NB: So you go about writing each book differently? You wrote NO *on that long sheet of paper . . .*

CM: Yeah.

NB: And you never did that again?

CM: I never did that again. And also I never had a clear vision of a book like that. *Reflex and Bone Structure* was a mock detective story or a kind of murder mystery and that's all I had in my mind, that I was going to do this very, very strange murder mystery. But I never knew from day to day where it was going. I would just sit there and say, "OK, typewriter, here I am" and that's the way I took it from day to day. In the subsequent drafts [it] became a lot clearer to me what I could do with it, but the first draft was a learning process, unlike it was for *NO.*

    And then the same is true all over again with *Emergency Exit.* It took seven, eight years to write that and during the first two years there were some very bleak moments when I did not know whether I'd be able to finish it. I had a vision of the whole thing as early as the second year, but I did not really know that I could pull it off.

There were times when I didn't believe I could do it. And so even with the vision, I wasn't able to do it the way that I did *NO* which was easy and spontaneous. It was a struggle and I had to throw away a lot; I had to rewrite and revise and reshape and pull parts out and reshuffle parts and all those kinds of really frustrating and aggravating things. I'm not able to say I have now enough experience to go forward and write my books . . .

NB: Easily.

CM: Because I don't. I can't really use the experience. It's not like an automobile mechanic who works on Volkswagens and he knows Volkswagens, so he's able to really use that knowledge and it carries over from car to car.

NB: So it really is a matter of starting over every day.

CM: And starting over every day with complete innocence, with no tools. It involves discovering a new approach with each time, with each step. I could write to a formula, and write the same book over and over. Some writers do that and I'm sure it's a lot easier and less aggravating. Probably they make more money doing that; but in the long run, I don't think it would be very satisfying to do the same book over and over with different names. I really welcome the challenge. I'm not knocking it; I think it's vital and it's the only way to attempt to write anything that has any vitality.

NB: Do you think that writing clarifies your sense of yourself?

CM: I'm sure that's true, but I'm not sure that it happens in the same way all the time; what I think happens is that very often you'll look back at something you wrote, say, a year ago or two years ago or maybe ten years ago, and understand something about yourself that you didn't understand while you were making that piece of writing. Or you become very aware in the very process. So the learning process, for me, is never the same. I just finished a book about the late actress Dorothy Dandridge who committed suicide in 1965. It's a fictional treatment of her life, but I discovered while writing the book, a lot of things about my own outlook, about my own experiences, my own attitudes and prejudices, everything, through the process of trying to project myself into her, into her sensibility, into her mind, into her outlook.

NB: In a couple of things I read, you seem to condemn social realism.

CM: Oh, I still think that. I think that. I don't think that I've fallen into that trap in writing this Dorothy Dandridge book. In a way, I don't want to say this too often, I think that it's really a book as much about myself as it is about Dorothy Dandridge. The average commercial reader would not want to hear a statement like that. That's the kind of thing that if it's true, it should not be there as an interference for the average reader. Writers are usually writerly readers, so it's OK to know that sort of thing. Even if it is an interference, it's OK because you can read the writing or you can read the story or you can read both at the same time. I think it's possible to make the language have a life of its own. This is what I think does not happen in realistic fiction.

NB: Because they're interested in . . .

CM: They're interested in the story and they want the language to be transparent; the language is supposed to be some sort of window through which you see the experience. But I think that realistic fiction that pays attention to the life of the language itself and which allows the story to move is vital and has a chance of lasting. There are a lot of good examples of that kind of fiction around today and have been for the last thirty–forty years. Saul Bellow, for example, I think, writes very writerly fiction, and it's also readerly. There are so many others I could name.

NB: It's hard for me to read experimental fiction and that upsets me because your comments on the limits of realistic fiction make sense to me. Something you said about poetry and prose may explain my problem: "The distinction I had made all along between poetry and prose I gradually realized was and has been a serious trap. For me, at least, it was false and it had been hanging me up. I came to see what I had been trying to do in making a novel was the same thing I meant to do in producing a poem." I can read poetry that's not narrative, because I expect that; but when I pick up a novel, I think "This is supposed to go a certain way," so when it doesn't go that way . . .

CM: Right. I'm forever bewildered by that. People can read poetry and accept the most incredible leaps of the imagination and the most incredible experimental things and they can also watch surrealistic movies; even Buster Keaton and Charlie Chaplin were very radical in terms of the visual experience and the kinds of things that they did with so-called reality. You can see it especially in Chaplin, in things like *Modern Times;* the audience has no problem accepting *Modern Times* on the screen and yet they cannot sit down with a novel like Bathelme's *The Dead Father,* for example, and read that with as much interest because . . . I think it has to do with conditioning; it has to do with what we expect of language. The primary problem is that language is the thing we use to relate to each other and therefore, it's forever changing and losing its stance and losing its ability to hold still. For instance, paint or ink on paper will stay pretty much the way it was put on paper for a long time. But language changes and so a book that was written 100 years ago becomes not only a literary experience when you read it, it's also a historical experience because that language is not our language anymore; though that ink on paper 100 years ago is still ink on paper today, so the experience hasn't been subjected to such an incredible change in our perception of the materials. Literature is unlike any art form because it has the problem of language as its material, and also the problem of our perception which is always gauged out of this thing we call reality.

NB: You've said things that imply to me that you believe in order to write anything original or interesting, you have to get as close to your perception of things as you can.

CM: I don't remember saying that, but it sounds true. *(Laughter.)* I would say that it's very complex and difficult because this whole idea of getting into yourself constitutes a problem because if you're writing from an intensive, personal, subjective point of view, you're also facing the inevitable problem of near-sightedness. You're very likely to miss something. One example: I was living in New York. I was walking along the street and passing in front of the laundromat and a dog was tied to the parking meter. A little girl came out of the laundromat to pet the dog and the dog bit off her ear. Whack! Just like that. A lot of people gathered around and it was a very tragic moment. It was not the thing you would expect on a casual afternoon; people were feeling good in the city; it was one of the first warm days. I tried to write a poem about it. I wanted to say something about how it affected me and what the implications were: how unsafe I felt we all were, forever. To try to put that on paper proved to be extremely difficult and finally, impossible. I was just too close to it. I tried to do it that very day. What we very often need is some distance, not just from the experience, but from ourselves, in order to write anything worthwhile.

That distance is very necessary and can be achieved in different ways. I think it's possible to do a first draft, for example, and put it away. Usually that's my process. I'll do a first draft of something and won't know how I feel about it. I'll put it away and look at it six months later, three weeks later, sometimes two years later, and then I can start working at the thing in some sort of objective way, so that I can see what's there in a way that I wasn't able to see in the beginning. But that's my process. I tend to overwrite and have to cut a lot, so usually what I do is look for the essence of it and try to refocus the thing and glean out whatever vitality might be there.

NB: You write a lot about letting things happen when you're writing. Is that what you're saying now? You let it happen and then you sift it?

CM: First of all, I put it on the paper to try to see what it is, because I don't know, and then when I can see what it's trying to be, I go back and I try to reshape it and impose a kind of order upon it and focus and direction. But I don't necessarily encourage my students to write that way. We're all individuals and we're all different. There are many, many ways in which things can be accomplished. What I try to do is understand their processes and it's really interesting for me to see all those different ways that things can be made, watching the students work.

NB: So you try to understand how they go about it and then reinforce whatever . . .

CM: Yeah, right. And I don't ever impose a group assignment, but I make assignments optional so that they can pick and choose because they work in different ways and on a different basis and it would be unreasonable to try to make them all in my image.

NB: Or encourage them to do anything in a certain way.

CM: Right. Except their way.

NB: That must be exhausting.

CM: It is, it is. *(Laughter.)*

NB: Someone else I've spoken with said that his students think that all good writing makes an important point and so they spend all their energy trying to think up a significant thesis. Have you seen that problem in your students?

CM: Well, that's very true of my students, especially the fiction writers. They will have an argument that they need to give expression to and they will build the story around the argument. There are different ways I go at that. There is a student in one of my classes now who writes really excellent satirical pieces about political situations and you can see that the fiction is really there as a kind of conveyer for this argument. Well, then you think, that's what the history of satire has always been, really. You look back to Swift; you look back to Nathaniel West. I think it's OK and probably works pretty well, and it certainly has a substantial history and tradition. But the other kind is a lot more aggravating, where the students really have some sort of muddled notion of what the point of view should be and so on and really try to decorate that idea with a few pages of careless prose. That's a lot more disturbing from my point of view.

NB: What do you do?

CM: I do several things, depending on the situation. *(Laughter.)* I would try the positive approach and try to find ways to use these pieces in different ways to discuss writing problems. But I run into the problem of so many students being in workshop who are there for approval rather than tough, hard criticism and that's one of the more difficult things that I have to face in dealing with the kinds of manuscripts that are, quote—not worth talking about—unquote. These people are paying as much as anyone else, so they deserve their money's worth. I try to find whatever is useful in these things to serve as an example for the whole class without alienating the person, but there is always that problem.

A great example: I once worked with a woman and she was a very careless writer. She was a very frustrated housewife and full of anger and wanted to get out into the world and feel her presence, which was fine; but she came into the workshop with the wrong kind of attitude: she wanted a support group rather than criticism. She wanted encouragement and hopefully, I do give encouragement; but she wanted enthusiastic response and she certainly deserved it, but she probably should have gone to a support group. Her writing was just embarrassingly bad.

And then there are people who feel like they want to spend the rest of their lives writing and they shouldn't do that. What do you tell them? And so those are the difficult, sensitive moments; but those situations don't present themselves very often because usually the student serious about writing will have enough self-knowledge, self-confidence and talent to know whether or not he can expect recommendations, etc., encouragement . . .

I don't believe that I can always help anyone become a better writer, but I think I can always help them become better readers and then become more sensitive to the language and how it's put together. They take that writerly experience back to the reading process; I've seen it happen. They understand something of the process and therefore, they can read with greater sensitivity, and more pleasure too.

There are three or four, five perhaps, in each class that are really good. I've worked with students who have published books over the years and who are now beginning to make names for themselves. So that's very satisfying and I like to think that I had some small part, anyway, in their development. There is so much talent, it's just incredible. I'm sure most of it will just go down the drain and will never develop and I'm sure that happens with every generation.

NB: Why? Because they don't need to write?

CM: Because they don't need to write. Very often you get someone without any talent at all.

NB: Who needs to write?

CM: Who needs to write *(laughter)*—and that person will hit the top of the best-seller list in five or six years. It happens all the time. It's OK; it's the way it should be, I suppose. Well, it's not the way it should be.

NB: *I gather from some of the things you've written that you're not*
very enthusiastic about people writing to make money.

CM: Well, I think that money from writing should be made acci-
dentally; I don't think you should plan it. I don't think a writer
should sit down and write a book for money; it's not a wholesome,
healthy motivation for writing poetry or fiction because . . . We have
a recent literary situation in this country and Europe as evidence of
that. All the worst things that Fitzgerald did he wrote for money.
All of his slap-dash stories for the *Saturday Review* aren't really
taken that seriously; every once in a while, a critic will say, "Well,
those stories are worth taking a look at again. They're not really so
bad." But they really are bad because they were manufactured pretty
much to a formula for money and compared to the kinds of things
Hemingway did with the short story . . . If you compare the two, you
can see how Hemingway allowed himself a greater sense of freedom
and certainly he started with a healthier motivation.

The problem in writing for money is that, almost without exception, one allows one's knowledge of the market to dictate the form
and direction of the work. And the market place and its notions of
how things ought to be, is invariably wrong or shallow or mediocre;
all those structures that have been tested, have proven to be sellable,
are the kinds of structures that editors and publishers try to insist
on.

NB: *What about the view that writing programs are irresponsible*
because they are staffed with people like you who don't want to teach
people how to make a lot of money writing, so you're taking money
from these people and giving them nothing.

CM: I believe in making money and I believe in making money
from writing. I know she's not a good example of a moneymaking
writer, *(laughter)* but Gertrude Stein said something that is very,
very fitting: She said that the writer should force the world to see
things his way rather than adapting himself to the outlook of the
world. I think you can address that statement to the conflict between
the editor and the writer: the editor wants the writer to adapt himself
to the formulas that have already proven successful, and she is
saying, on the other hand, that the successful writer is a writer who
invents a new way of seeing the world rather than simply imitating

the old tested ways of seeing the world. I think it's possible to make money Gertrude Stein's way . . . Well, Hemingway certainly made a lot of money. I can think of a lot of excellent writers who made a lot of money; Dickens made a lot of money.

NB: In the introduction to your collection, The New Black Poetry, *you said, "Unlike most contemporary white poets, we are profoundly conscious of forces that ironically protect us from the empty patterns of intellectual gentility and individualism and at the same time keep our approach fresh." It seems to me that the intellectual gentility doesn't produce that many writers; at least, I don't think many of the people I've spoken with would see themselves as products of the intellectual gentility, nor would they be seen that way by others.*

CM: Well, it's probably true, for the most part, but it's also strange, isn't it, because writers always, until very recently, came from the upper classes. They were the only ones who had any time to write or even think about writing or doing any of the arts. There are few exceptions to that: Millet, for example, who was a peasant and on the doorstep of starvation half the time and I'm sure there are others; but, yeah, the social changes that have taken place since the French Revolution probably turned the whole world upside down. The kinds of suffering that people from the lower classes or lower-middle classes perceive, I think, really became more vital in terms of their implications in art than the kinds of perceptions that were coming from the upper classes.

My wife is working on her dissertation and she has done a lot of research on myth, ritual and metaphor, also on the early Spanish picaresque novel and by watching over her shoulder, I've learned that the early picaresque novel is almost without exception about the downtrodden, the vagabonds, or the outsiders. These books were written by people from the upper classes; even that early, the kinds of perceptions made from the lower depths, so to speak, about thieves and prostitutes and so on, were considered even then, four or five hundred years ago, as perhaps more vital or at least more interesting. That was certainly the forerunner, I think, of the modern novel.

NB: Someone I talked to suggested that in order to have anything to say, you have to put yourself in different social contexts; you have to put yourself in situations where you see things from a new angle.

CM: I think that's very true. I don't think you can feel safe and write any vital fiction. I think you have to place yourself in a position where a lot of forces are at work. As I say this, I'm also aware in the back of my head of all kinds of exceptions to this rule. I think about the fact that Reubens, the painter, was a comfortable middle-class man in politics and did some remarkable paintings. And William Carlos Williams was a baby doctor who never went without money. On the other hand, Modigliani was walking through alleys practically feeding himself out of garbage cans. So I think great art can come from any class, but I think it's a nice idea that one has to suffer in a garret somewhere in order to produce a great piece. It's probably true for a large number of people and it's certainly true for me. For many years I was living a dangerous kind of existence. I lived in New York for twelve years; I was not in the safe world of the university with a nice insurance policy and tenure and all those very nice things, so I was constantly working out from that place of insecurity. You can't argue with your own experience; it's there! But I don't think you can generalize.

NB: I have a couple of paragraphs of yours here that I didn't under-stand completely. The first one is: "See all this heavy disenchantment spreading through the early 1970s? It came from well-composed minds. People go mad only because they begin from something called logic. You have to be saved. And the way is through the lingo of magic understanding and a trust in the Dark and Feeling. They inter-change."

CM: Wow! You want me to comment on that? Actually, what I was saying, I think, in simple language, is that one should trust one's instincts and if you're a writer, if you're trying to make a work of art out of prose or poetry, you have to go with your instincts. Follow them and you can use that knowledge that is there. It knows more than we know.

NB: And when people with well-composed minds order things, it twists everything?

CM: Yeah.

NB: Then the next paragraph says, "You can call it political action *if you wanna but you get turned around, trapped in match and the spell of Rap. Dark and Feeling have moved nations since the beginning of man's reaction to woman's awesome ability to give birth to man and woman. It's how civilization began."*

CM: Well, I got carried away. *(Laughter.)* But anyway, it's still about that trust of instinct, but I was getting at this whole thing about the woman being at the root of all . . . Nobody knows for sure, but it's one of my beliefs that there were, before recorded history, cultures in which women were either equal or leaders and I'd like to believe that those cultures were better than ours in some ways, that the people in those cultures were in touch with themselves in a way that we have not been because of our male-oriented cultures. If I had any religion, I don't have any religion, actively, but it's one of my pet peeves . . . The world probably would have been better off had women maintained their earlier stance. I think of it as a conspiracy, the whole arrival of civilization, as the act that put men in power, that made woman powerless.

NB: Why?

CM: Let me see if I can articulate it. I think that probably men set up systems in which they were able to gain some security at the expense of women. They had to establish their relationship with their god and in order to build that and to sustain that, they had to subject women to a kind of servitude; they had to create a distance between themselves and women in order to sustain their own identities and to create the false security that has always underscored their existence. And I think this happened because women were mysterious; they were associated with all these mysterious things like blood and birth . . .

NB: I think I read this in Emergency Exit.

CM: Oh, was this in *Emergency Exit?* Yeah, well I think that's where it all stemmed from; I think it all came out of that need to put that mystery at a distance and keep it under control. And in order to keep it under control, women had to be reduced socially.

Now how the conspiracy took place has been dealt with by several different kinds of researchers, anthropologists, historians, and so on. The act of conspiracy took place as a result of cultural factors like the mastery of writing, for example, or the making of picture language, which gave men—I don't know why men were the ones to create it, but they were—a kind of weapon for controlling and manipulating women. Levi-Strauss thinks language is the turning point, the invention of language. There are some researchers who believe that conspiracy evolved in the nature of language as a weapon rather than to be used in art, even the art of cave drawings of animals. All of that inspired language, too, in a sense. That's the kind of language I'm talking about. Earlier than that even, just magical utterings of some early tribal people. It's all also connected with metaphor and myth too; all of that is interwoven in the sense that the process of looking at an object and establishing a relationship between that object and a sound, for example, metaphor in that very primitive sense. Now why that should have been the property of men, I don't know. And I'm not altogether convinced that it was solely the property of men in those early tribal cultures except in the sense that it was used as conspiracy.

I remember one tribe that I read about had the practice of taking boys who were ready for the puberty rites . . . The men would take them out into the forest and would tell the women that they were going to take the boys to listen to God. And then they would tie a rock on a string and swing it around and the motion made a very loud, bizarre sound that the women could hear back in the village and they were told that that was the voice of God and that the boys were being introduced to God and therefore, they were privileged. That God is a metaphor and it's also language. So in that sense, that was the private property of men; women were not privileged to speak the language of God. And in early Christian cultures, man was made in God's image. I hadn't made those connections before this moment. Really, I'm not sure, but I think there might be something there.

NB: A large number of the people I've spoken with talk about the importance of having their students read aloud and listen to their writing. Is that . . .

CM: Yeah, I think so. Especially in poetry, but also in fiction. I will have certain kinds of prose read in class because they lend themselves to that kind of expression; it's not just a visual experience. I certainly learn a lot by reading my work in public; it's a way of educating myself in public, or not educating myself, but rewriting, which is an educational process. And a way of getting distance too, looking at my work from different angles. Very often right in front of an audience, I will make a mental note to change something I'm reading because I've suddenly had the experience of seeing what's wrong with it as I'm reading it. So I think it's important.

NB: One article I read suggested having the students talk into tape recorders and then write from that material. The author said he thought that would make what they wrote more honest because people tend to lie when they write.

CM: They only think of writing as an approximation of their speech and the extent of our normal experience with writing is to write a letter to someone and it's not really the same. It's always the same tired, worn-out expressions: "Dear Betty, I'm sorry that I didn't write earlier . . . ," rather than doing it the way we would speak. We get into the habit of thinking that writing cannot be an instrument of the voice, but the most effective writing always has been an approximation of the voice. I'm always trying to get students to write in their own voices and also to write out of their experiences and to write about what they know about and part of that process involves using an approximation of their own speech, not the way Shakespeare wrote and talked.

NB: That sounds good. I had a student last year who used inflated language, because he was scared, I guess, and when he came to my office, I had him read his paper out loud. He knew right away what the problem was.

CM: I run into it all the time with students who will get fascinated with a certain writer and they'll be writing that writer's prose. That's fine as a learning process, but one should move beyond that and constantly think in terms of moving toward one's own voice and one's own speech and one's own rhythms. That idiom is a vital part of the experiences they should be writing about.

Most students in college today aren't going to have an opportunity to be in touch with who they are and where they come from in such an intense way ever again as they will in a workshop. They will go into different kinds of things: business, engineering, the sciences; but hopefully, they will remember how important it was to create a wedding of that voice that was theirs and that history that was theirs. No matter how much television one watches or how many movies one watches, the kinds of associations produced by those kinds of experiences remain marginal and accidental and incidental; they won't be like the experience of writing and discovering one's voice and creating that bridge to an audience. That's an entirely unique experience that there is no substitute for.

FREDERICK MANFRED

FM: Poems come out like angleworms: if you pull them out right, they come out perfect. A poem is put together by the dreamer in you; I don't know if it's way downstairs in the basement or way up in the attic, but wherever it is, it's all been gone over and organized. I hardly ever rewrite a poem. I'll rearrange the stanzas once in a while, although I'm beginning to question that; I should probably leave them just the way they come out. The right side of my brain is kicking those out and the left side is trying to organize them. You feel with your right side. Your left side makes you logical, social and so on; you have to be suspicious of that.

Novel writing is a completely different operation. There you can be an amateur architect and amateur carpenter. You're making a long report on a certain activity in society and that takes a long time to get organized. You worry about plot and structure and, at the same time, you're trying to suck up as much as you can from the basement or the attic. I generally have a plot worked out, a target area, because I have a tendency to digress. But if something occurs in the story that asks me to take a side path or some new person comes popping in, I welcome it and follow that; just so I get at that target area.

I rub my hands in glee whenever I hit a wall in my manuscript and I don't know where to go next. There's a damn good reason why: it's something I don't want to look at. If I can push through and get into that area, I'll find something not only about myself, but something that may be of real value to someone else. And inadvertently, everything you need, the theme, the plot, will jump right out at you as you go along. Mark Twain's *Pudd'nhead Wilson* started off being one thing and then wound up two stories; I think that makes that a very powerful novel although he should have spent more time putting all that together. He should have explored what pulled him off base. Mark Twain was a forerunner; I wish he had done more exploring of himself, but he spent too much time lecturing.

Madison Jones and I had some great talks and we remarked that we often write the novel we're next going to live out. For example, if I were to write about a roué, after the book is done, I might start chasing women. *(Laughter.)* And that's a curious thing: I did that somewhat with *Milk of Wolves.* I found myself being interested in a lot of women after I wrote that book. *(Laughter.)*

NB: You've said that as you write more your dreams improve.

FM: Yeh. The only thing you've got to be careful with is that pretty soon you self-instruct your dreamer. You want those dreams to come up naturally.

NB: Do you record your dreams?

FM: I got probably a hundred dreams I've typed up in the last six or seven years. I write them down the next day. The only ones I record are those I remember. I figure there's a reason why you remember it, just like there's a reason you never forget certain incidents in your life. Those are the ones you should write about.

NB: You also read a lot of philosophy. Do you worry about that creeping into your stories?

FM: No, it stimulates me and widens my brain and allows me to receive more. It rarely shows up in my novels. It might in my poetry because philosophy can pop into poetry quite easily; if it's done beautifully, it's very powerful. But fiction is fiction. I'm highly suspicious of authors who preach in their novels. I have trouble reading Saul Bellow; his stuff is often animated essay—which maybe is all right for the academic critic, but it's not really fiction. True fiction is where the reader, no matter what the intelligence is, gets lost in the story. You can relay profound information by the route of fiction; it's a philosophical inquiry in story form. The findings in fiction are just as legitimate as those made by a logical route and you shouldn't mix them up.

Homer wouldn't have been repeated orally for two, three, four hundred years if there had been a lot of philosophy or moral instruction in it. It was a great story. When you're sitting over the campfire after a hard day's work in a war campaign, or conquering a new area, you don't want heavy sermons. You want a good story while you're drinking your mead or gnawing away at a roast. A good story is basic to human enjoyment, so I go for the story line. It isn't that I don't have any philosophical thoughts: I'm always booting them out when they try to sneak into my stuff. If a character wants to talk it, I won't give him much more than seven, eight lines, and then I'm going to interrupt him with some jackass talking so it doesn't get too heavy. I'm not going to let him take over.

I won't let myself get in there. I write in my journals and I occasionally give talks. March 31st I gave a talk to USD about two things. One is that science is making a terrible mistake by thinking that there is such a thing as Time. The other argument I suggested was that maybe the final indivisible building block of the universe, whether particle or wave, may be a piece of life not the way we conceive of it, but of another kind that informs both organic and inorganic matter, something I call a deon. So it isn't that I don't do a lot of that kind of thinking, but unless I get a scientist in there, it'll never show up in my books.

NB: Fiction writers in particular have talked about the importance of being exposed to different ways of seeing things. Why?

FM: It's a mind stretcher, a mental muscle stretcher and at the same time a mental muscle builder. It gives you more options. It's a little like in baseball. If you're a pitcher, you do all kinds of stretching and running and fooling around with different pitches on the sidelines and in training period; but when the game is on, you concentrate on the one pitch to be made with the batter standing in there ready to hit your ball. If you think about all those theories at the moment you wind up, you're licked. A real athlete always operates instinctively; all that previous training and previous experience will show up automatically. And it's fun. That kind of mental play keeps your mind active and alive. Anything to keep that muscle upstairs alive and full of tensile strength helps you write fiction. That's early morning stuff, isn't it?

NB: You've talked about writers being especially nice people: "The highest a man can become is to be one of these artists. It's true that they look a little foolish to other people because they happen to be so plainspoken and because they take strong positions. But this is because they somehow manage to keep a child's innocence while looking for truth." Why do you think artists are like this?

FM: Unfortunately, Harry Stack Sullivan died a rather young man in a car accident, but he was on the way to becoming our American Freud before he got whacked and he had some marvelous things to say about writers. He felt that if mankind as a species is driving towards some ideal state of being, then all men and all women will have artistic natures. And there are hints of it already in our society. When you run into a middle class family that has aspirations for itself, let's say it's a legal family, you'll find that the older sons or daughters will be interested in law, or that general field, and do well financially and socially. But when it comes to the youngest child, the family will say, "Oh, he's terribly bright. It looks like he's going to be our artist." And then they push him and hope he's going to be the family star. This is also true of aristocratic families and poor families. So behind the facade of trying to get along, there is a secret hope in everyone that "my child is going to be special; if not a president, then maybe a Mr. Faulkner or a Charles Ives or Frank Lloyd Wright." So there's a motion in our race towards having us become a special species.

Every writer I've run into of any consequence—Robert Penn Warren, Bellow, Bly, McGrath, Lewis, Dos Passos, Fisher, Waters, Walter Clark—were all strong people with strong egos and strong drives and strong bodies. And almost in every case they felt a little odd in youth. I knew I was different from people around me. I had to nourish that and keep it alive all the while that I hid it. Because if you don't hide it you get lampooned by your buddies and by your hundred IQers. The average person didn't understand you and thought that you wrote because you were slightly crazy. But you knew better. You knew for your intelligence this was normal activity.

NB: You've said that people drink because they want to be high like an artist when he is going good; but according to legend, writers drink a lot.

FM: There's occasionally a writer who drinks. People who can't write latch on to this and say, "I'm not a great writer; but the reason he is, is that he drinks." Beach had the theory that a writer was like an oyster: if a grain of sand got in there, a pearl will develop. Something bothered him, so he wrote. Well, to begin with that's not so. I say you write because you are a superior being. This is arrogance, but I consider it permissible arrogance since that's part of who you are as a writer. You write because it's a natural thing to flower in that way, just like the male bird sings near the nest where the female is sitting on the eggs to let everybody know: "Hey, this is my area," and also, "Say, this is pretty nice. I'm singing away here and I really like it." That's why writers or artists explode into song: it's possessive, as well as a giveaway.

NB: Do you think writers could drink when they miss the high of writing well?

FM: I guess Hemingway did near the end of his life. Hemingway didn't drink in the morning when he was writing though. And Faulkner drank in between books; he had to have his head clear when he wrote. I always felt that the "fifth" I can't understand in Faulkner is Mr. Jack Daniels. There's no question that drinking alcohol in between those writing bouts affected his brain. Something happens to your brain after you drink enough alcohol: those synapses are slowly but surely being relaxed and dulled by alcohol, and writing comes out of the wonderful work of your synapses in your associative centers. So you want to have a healthy brain and healthy body so your synapses and your associative centers are sparking away like hell.

But there are just as many bankers who drink as there are writers. The day John Berryman jumped off the bridge near the University of Minnesota, a vice president of the First National Bank also jumped off the bridge a little further up the river. John Berryman got the front page in the second section; the other guy got an obituary in the back. That's not fair. That's pointing and saying, "Oh, he jumped because he's a crazy artist." What about that crazy banker? You can't say that artists are inclined to be more neurotic or eccentric or drunken or apt to have more divorces than any other man in other business.

In my social schema, there are two classes of people: artistocrats, who are creative people, and the rest, who try to be. If there are any kings and queens they are creative people. But they shouldn't take on airs. From the point of view of a worm, two human beings standing above the worm, one of them a moron, the other an Einstein, look exactly alike to the worm. If there is a God, from the point of view of God, Einstein and the moron also look equally bright. So you shouldn't take on prima donna airs. If you're really good, you don't have airs. Einstein didn't have airs; Hardy didn't; Warren doesn't.

NB: Some people have suggested that having airs would get in the way of your writing.

FM: Of course. That's a bit like the pitcher who's got great stuff: fast balls, great curves, changeups, powerful physique, quick as a cat, can field grounders. If, just as he's about to pitch, he remembers the story in the paper about him four days ago when he pitched a two-hitter, he's going to get knocked out of the box. He isn't going to be concentrating on his next pitch. He's got to be totally lost in the moment of that action. He can't be thinking about his press clippings. It's the same way with a writer: he's got to be lost in the moment of writing; he can't be thinking that he's a genius.

NB: The people I've talked to have been very nice, but when I say that to other people, they say it's because I've only talked to people who've succeeded.

FM: I was at the Huntington Hartford Foundation twice. We had four categories: sculpture, painting, music, and writing. None of it was criticism. Everything had to be original. There were four to a category, two older people and two younger ones. There was some rivalry, but less than I found in any other business. The early part of the day, you are supposed to leave each other alone. But in the evening, everyone met in the commons for dinner, and one of the first questions invariably was, "Did you have a good day?" Not that silly American expression, "Have a good day," but, "Did you really write well today?" Or, "Did you sculpt well today? How did it go? Did you make something new? Can we look at it?" We all hoped that everyone would do well. They know if they do something well and if somebody else also does something well, life will be richer for each of us. I've wished a Shakespeare was living in my home town of Luverne, Minnesota. He'd be greater than me, at least possibly *(laughter),* but my life would be richer.

NB: You've said, "The ideal life is to find what's there and then to live with it." Do you think writers are better at that than other people?

FM: They're more apt to be. You learn more about yourself and then you learn how to put that down, whereas the other fellow is so busy being a social being that he won't learn that. You run into a man who is in business—it takes a long time to figure out who he really is. He's doing everything in relation to that business: will it sell, will it not sell? Will this hurt me in the community, or won't it hurt me? He's continually concerned about front room stuff, not back room stuff. That doesn't work for a writer.

NB: So how do you teach your students to be writers?

FM: I had a great teacher in philosophy, Dr. Harry Jellema at Calvin College. He always gave you a chance and he made it a game every day. It was always a thrill to go to that class. One day he started the class reading my story, "A Harvest Scene," out of *The Chimes.* And the kids in the class all started looking at me. I always sat by the window. I could feel my face being bombarded by these pairs of eyes. I looked out the window so I wouldn't see the eyes. I was thrilled and excited and embarrassed. When he got all done, he explained why he read it: that it had such and such meanings, and what it meant in relation to such and such a philosophy. And he did that with every kid in the class. It was marvelous to have that happen to you. It didn't give you the big head; it just made you think, "Say, I'm not half bad." He was a great teacher.

I try to run my writing class the way Jellema ran his Plato Club, which was not a class but a philosophy club. Every member had to give a paper before the end of the year. That was your night. You handed out copies of your paper to the members a week or two ahead of time, so everybody could read it, and when you arrived, you read it again. You spent the whole night thrashing out the ideas in the paper and the other things we ran across as we argued and talked. It started out at seven and might go on until two in the morning. It was the best "class" I ever had because it was informal and that's how I modeled my writing classes.

In turn, I hope that every one of those kids in my class, if they become teachers, run their class like I ran it. I think teaching would be a lot better. But I should make an observation here. I don't have much time for psychologists and psychiatrists. Their field is a new field; it's also a tough field to explore because you can't point at a particle like you can in science. They tend to be defensive, so they'll take dictums by Freud and Jung and Adler and Horney and then talk as if those things are actually there—when they're not really there: they're just super guesses. We've got about twenty thousand practicing psychiatrists in the country applying these critical apparati and trying to make their patients fit these categories rather than the other way around: listen to what the patient has to say and see what the patient really is and work from there. In the first instance you're doing it as a practitioner and as a kind of teacher, and in the second you're doing it as an artist. There can't be that many artists around; there can't be twenty thousand geniuses around, all located in the field of psychiatry. Well, the same in teaching. You have to be highly talented to be a good teacher and there aren't that many highly talented persons around in any society at any time, so to ask almost a million teachers to be artists is hard going. So you thank God that the few good ones did go into the teaching profession because they're handing something from one generation to another.

NB: In The Wind Blows Free *you said you didn't want to become a teacher because teachers get dried up and over particular. Why do you think that happens?*

FM: Because they're overworked. I love teachers. Teachers and librarians are terribly necessary to society. These days those people are continually overworked. But I for myself can't stand repetition. So every year I try to teach my small class different. And that's important to a creative writer: that you have to be new all the time. A writer . . . you don't say "have to"; if you say, "have to," that means you're already lost. You are continually being new. It's no wonder the average teacher is dried up. Even the genius teacher finds that his classes are too large.

NB: What do you want your students to get from your classes?

FM: At least this, that after they get out of school, even if they don't write, they will know how a poem or a story is put together. If they should happen to be teachers later on, say TAs, they're that much the better comp teachers. If they teach later on the advanced creative writing course, they'll know how to teach that too. They won't come wandering in from some other discipline and try to get it from a book. They have seen an author at work.

What a joy and inspiration it would have been to me if, when I was a young man at Calvin College, I could have seen Sinclair Lewis walking across the campus once a week: how he walked and how he looked, and how he looked at the rose bushes and the girls. *(Laughter.)* We learn best by watching examples around us. Little boys imitate their fathers and little girls imitate their mothers. So it's the same way with young writers imitating . . . although I tell them that they got to figure out their own way of doing something. I always tell them, "If you resist me, privately I'll admire you, provided you convince me you know what you're doing." This is not the usual English class where they have to curry a prof's favor. Once in a while they catch me up short in something, or I've overlooked something, or made the wrong observation. I always say, "By golly, I think you're right." I don't get on any high horse.

I might tell you how I run the class.

NB: Okay.

FM: I have these exercises I want them to go through first, and then they're to have one overall project. What we want at the end is an excellence inside of what they can do. The first thing they turn in is an autobiography because I like to know where they're from. They can write that in any form they want, just so I know how old they are, what their parents were like, if they have brothers and sisters, if there have been any deaths, if they're married, if they're embittered or not embittered, and so on. That's absolutely confidential and I return that to them.

Then I want to see a letter to their best friend that's not aimed at me; not a letter they write after they've met me. Same way with a page from their journal, if they keep a journal. And a dream, if possible one as soon as the class has started because that dreamer in the back of your head might aim a dream at me too. If possible try to remember an old dream and get that down without thinking about style; try to plop it down as it occurs to you because a real dream has odd qualities: it isn't logical, wanders in all directions, people change clothes without reason, faces change, bodies change, and I want all that. See, I'm already suggesting some powerful forces at work. They have to be aware I might be bending them a little bit.

Then they must write an opening paragraph, whether they are fiction writers or not, and we compare it to the opening paragraphs of *Islands in the Stream* or *A Farewell to Arms* and we talk about whether if you were to pick up a book in a bookstore with that opening paragraph, would that catch your eye?

Then they're supposed to keep their ears cocked for lively and interesting conversation around them and try to get that down, whether it's in the women's room or in the men's room or the student union or at home or in a hospital. Put it all down; don't try to edit it; just stick it down; and we'll help cut it in class and show how sometimes two pages can be condensed to four exchanges and you still have it all.

By the time they're through with all this, I get a pretty good idea of what their forte is, and they learn that writing is not getting on a literary horse, that literature is something that comes out of you spontaneously. The reason we think Steinbeck's style is good is because this is his natural way of talking. And Hemingway, too. And what we want to find is a natural way of doing things. And then we can go to town. Not that I can teach them anything, but that the class is there for them to explore their potential.

They oftentimes say, "What can we write about?" I tell them, if there is some memory that keeps recurring to you, there's a deep reason for it. Explore it and then you'll have everything: you'll have the theme and the whole business sitting in there. If you're human and you've got brains and you're somewhat sane, it's going to be OK.

We do it altogether. As fast as I can, I get them to operate as a peer group. After a while, they start calling me Fred and I'm just a guy with them. And just as in Jellema's philosophy club, the Plato Club, each member of the class has to come up with a final project, which the others have a chance to read beforehand, and has it examined from stem to stern, and by me. Wonderful discussions follow each read project. By the end of the semester, everybody has got tears in their eyes because they have to let up. It's true. I had the

last class this past Monday and everybody was sitting there kind of
hating to get up because . . . why, they interrupt each other in a
friendly warm way and they all cheer when somebody gets tough
about his own things or tough about somebody else's. It's a friendly,
warm, but strong exchange.

NB: Why do you think that's so important to them?

FM: Because they can talk anyway they want; can be themselves
totally. They can't do it anywhere else.

When they're through with the class, you hope that they're on the
way to becoming superior citizens. They've learned to find out who
they are and what they can do and to do it enthusiastically. In that
sense, it's of great value that you have only twelve or fourteen people
in a class a year. Those twelve or fourteen people can be a power
wherever they go.

*NB: What do you think would happen if there were more teaching
like that?*

FM: It would revolutionize our country. I've had roughly 150
students. Suppose forty of those wound up in Congress, one-half in
the House of Representatives and one-half in the Senate. You can
imagine how odd they'd look to the other Senators who are always
worrying about their constituency. They'd speak their minds on the
theory that if their constitutents don't like what they say, they can
always not vote for them the next election. But I think the constit-
uents like to have a man or woman representative who really votes
how he feels. If they've elected him, they'll tend to trust him, especially if he or she is very honest.

NB: In Green Earth, *the principal tells Free that when he reads
more and his taste gets more sophisticated, he'll realize that Joseph
Conrad is a better writer than Mark Twain. Do you know where that
kind of prejudice comes from? For instance, I was just editing the
transcripts of interviews with three entirely different kinds of novelists
and they all mentioned Dickens in a favorable way. And a couple of
novelists have used Conrad as a bad example. While it seems to me
that academics tend to favor . . .*

FM: Conrad.

NB: And fiction writers talk about Dickens.

FM: Yeh, I would too. Conrad really bothers me. I've always had trouble reading him. But I finally figured out why. He was a Pole; he felt as a Pole. Then he was a Frenchman for a while; he learned to express himself in a clear logical way as a Frenchman. And then later on he became an Englishman. So he's working his way through three writing frames: feels as a Pole, thinks as a Frenchman, and writes as an Englishman. You're getting three languages coming at you in the guise of one: English. Something in you as a reader is picking up those two other echoes and throwing you off. By the time he writes his last book, it's almost pure English. He didn't have too much to say by that time, but that's the best written book from the point of view of a complete expression in one language. I worry a little about him; he was too intellectual even though he tried not to be. I think that's why critics latch onto him. Critics are not really the best critics *(laughter)* because they go at it as critics and not either as readers or as novelists.

NB: Oh, and so they want an ideological scheme.

FM: That's right. Actually critics should be the novelists because they are so busy bringing up marvelous critical apparati.

NB: Why aren't they novelists? What's the difference?

FM: They don't know how to play, literally play. They don't know how to play in their heads. That word "play" is a rich word.

NB: You've mentioned that it was probably good for Faulkner, Steinbeck, and Hemingway not to have much schooling: "I think college and graduate school is for the critical teacher, but if you are creative something goes wrong there, even if you have the most marvelous teacher in the United States. Something goes wrong in that critical atmosphere in the classroom." I don't quite understand what you're saying there because I don't see why a classroom atmosphere has to be critical.

FM: It tends to be, though. I had an English teacher at Calvin who was a wonderful reader when he read Shelley or Wordsworth. He had a kind of English accent. And gee, he didn't sound like anybody where I came from. When you're just a boy coming off the farm, or a boy coming out of the city working class, and you hear your prof say, "He had this in mind, or that was his purpose," you think to yourself, "Is it possible he knew all that before he began to write? I don't have that happen to me when I begin to write a short story, so I guess I can never be a novelist." It crushes you to hear all that stuff. But if you hadn't heard it, you wouldn't know that you couldn't do it, so you go ahead and do it. There's something about listening to profs who themselves will never write, who are a little envious probably, and who yet hide under the skirts of their genius: just like the disciples of Christ made him an overpowering world figure, they will make their favorite genius an overpowering person. That scares the hell out of your students, "I'll never be able to be that good."

In the beginning, you're like a little oak shoot, easily burned off, frozen off. An oak has to be a good twenty years old before it really will take hold and go, and it's the same with writers. It's like with an oak: if that little oak shoot could see the big oak, it'd say, "My God, I'll never get to be as big as that big oak sitting over there who knows how to resist storms and critical attention."

NB: Does teaching interfere with your writing?

FM: Yeh, it does. It takes a day away from my writing each week. Except in the summers. I would probably have had two more novels out by now; maybe even three. I will write them in the future. Luckily, the good Lord, or whatever, is going to give me many years of clarity and vigor, so I'll get in what I've intended to do.

I have wondered sometimes if that operation of being a boss—boss in quotes—of a class, doesn't make me possibly a little pontifical when I start writing and I worry a little bit about that.

When I drive to work in the morning, I turn my whole brain around to that day: how I'm going to handle that class and the people I'm probably going to see and the lunch I'm going to have. Then, when the class is over, as I drive home, I try to wash it all out so that the next morning I can go to work and forget the whole thing until the following Sunday afternoon. So far it's worked. But if I did any more of it, it would probably start pushing into the writing activity. You have only so much energy and so much eye (I) time. That's a pun, *e-y-e* and capital *I.*

Walter Clark regretted in some ways he had taught so much; he lost books to it. He only had four books printed. It's too bad he was pulled into the academic world; we lost a lot of wonderful books in Walter.

NB: We've probably gotten some good things from his students.

FM: That's true, yeh. But I don't know if they're going to get up to where Walter was. You got Walter ... why take a chance on someone who might never become a Walter? It takes ten thousand good student writers to find one good Walter. You have new ones coming in, but once you got a Walter, goddamn it, society should see to it that he has time and leisure to give us some books.

NB: Have you ever supported yourself doing anything else?

FM: I was a newspaper man before I went into teaching, and I worked in *Modern Medicine,* a medical magazine.

NB: Did those jobs interfere more or less with your writing than teaching?

FM: More. Newspapering was good for me for a while because I had to say things succinctly. But if you did it long enough, you wound up with non-metaphorical writing, and you also tended to load everything in the first two paragraphs rather than keep it for the climax. In medical writing you use a lot of polysyllabic words, which I always argue are nonfiction words. I throw them out. Einstein once made the remark that if you can't say something in simple terms that the average man can understand, you probably didn't have a clear thought in the first place. If you have to use heavy words to explain something, you probably don't understand it in the first place. The polysyllabic word is the hiding place of the uncertain brain.

NB: What do you get from teaching?

FM: Well, it paid bills; that's the left side of the brain talking. *(Laughter.)* Meeting fresh young minds, I have to learn how to be with them and how to handle them and understand them. There's a continual stretching of human tolerance and it enriches my ability to pick up new experiences that come willy-nilly at me.

NB: Why is writing the highest of the arts?

FM: I used to think music was. In the beginning I was affected more by a passage of music than I was by a passage in writing. Had

I had somebody around me who knew music and could detect musical talent, I might have been a composer today instead of a writer. I probably write more as a composer than I do as a real writer. I can always tell, for example, when someone has cut one word out of my text. It's as if they've lost a note on me.

But now that I've written all these books, I've come to the thought that perhaps the art of writing is not only the oldest, it's the most enriching. Music, after all, is narrow. It's just sounds. You can get a musical sound that suggests, "I love you," but only after you've learned to think "I love you" in language. Writing gives the reader or the person who wants to enjoy something in the world of art the most reward because not only do they get something out of the prose and style and rhythm of it, but they get an enormous amount of life in it.

JAMES ALAN McPHERSON

(This interview was not tape recorded at the request of James Alan McPherson. It is based on notes.)

NB: Your writing emphasizes the importance of seeing the limits of established orders and common assumptions. How does that idea influence your teaching?

JM: I try to have them read things which represent other traditions. For instance, I'll have them read something like Issac Babel and then I'll make statements that disturb them and make them think. It's important for the students to become aware of and challenge their assumptions because this country has bought into a false mythology. For example, basic American values evolved during three hundred years of Southern history, but we've turned our backs on that and embraced the myth of the American West. The West was a significant part of our history for only twenty-six years, from 1870 to 1896. We now have a people whose imaginations have been conditioned by the false mythology of the West. They're blind. The country's sense of itself is minuscule and the young people are heirs to this. They need to know there are other realities. I tell all the people from the suburbs [Arlington and Fairfax] to get out of my class. I'm kidding, but I refuse to deal with suburban angst. There are more important things to think about.

NB: A lot of people I've spoken with have talked about encouraging their students to be honest.

JM: I want my students to be cunning. We live in a world shaped by a fallacious folklore. If you're honest, you might get killed. Be-

83

sides, if you make direct statements, you become an ideologue, not a writer. Indirection persuades people more effectively than direct statement. For instance, Lenny Bruce and Richard Pryor use humor to attack routinized behavior and it works.

NB: What happens to your writing when you teach?

JM: I write less because I give all to my teaching. I have a tremendous amount of office hours with students. It takes all my time because as long as I'm doing something, I don't like to do a bad job.

I have to back away from it every once in a while. Everybody has an ego and everybody wants to be remembered. A teacher can't help but hope that maybe one of the students will remember something from class. And the temptation is to try to become a god in the classroom. I think the temptation to become a god is particularly strong for teachers of literature. It's important to become aware of and resist that temptation because students have impressionable minds. The power to open young minds is dangerous.

NB: What about the other jobs you listed in Railroads: *waiter, salad girl?*

JM: Oh, I was fooling around then. I was just showing there's nothing wrong with saying you're a Harvard graduate and a salad girl in the same breath.

NB: Were you able to write when you were a student at Harvard Law School?

JM: Sure. I went to Harvard from Savannah, Georgia and discovered that there were people at Harvard who were pleased to do something for blacks. One of those people was Thomas Crooks, the director of the Harvard Summer School. Every April and May, I'd go to him and say I needed to borrow money to go to Summer School and take writing courses. He'd always get it for me. He had no idea that I'd become a writer, but he was happy to do something for me. The danger of being someplace like Harvard is that you can O.D. on optimism. I kept my sanity by working as a janitor near Harvard Square at the same time that I was a student at Harvard Law.

NB: The kind of thinking a law student does seems different from what a writer does.

JM: Well, I've used law in my writing. For instance, I see a close analogy between the legal forms I learned about in Civil Procedure and literary form and that idea is central to my story, "A Sense of Story." But I didn't just want to be a lawyer. I learned things from going to law school, but I wanted to learn and see more things than that and I've decided that the literary imagination offers the broadest and most inclusive point of view. A few years after I left Harvard, I ran into Paul Freund who was my constitutional law professor at Harvard. He said he's been following my work and he thought I'd gone beyond the law. That makes me proud because Paul Freund himself has an amazing grasp of the interrelationships of things. He not only understands constitutional law, he understands the dynamics behind it. People at Harvard Law School are proud of John Casey and me because we went on to become writers.

NB: What about the notion that fiction is escapist and thin compared to nonfiction?

JM: All I know is that when I want solace, I can always find it in literature. How many people are still reading Mailer's "The White Negro"? But people are still reading Cervantes. There's nothing like the literary imagination.

NB: Do you think people can become writers by going to school?

JM: There's a wonderful writer named Bill Fox who makes these one word summaries. For instance, he'd say, "The secret of Southern cooking is grease." You're not going to get a Bill Fox coming out of Harvard writing about Proust. Good writing comes from hard experience. In school you learn Proust, but you don't get any experience. People at Harvard have gotten there by going through schools like the Bronx High School of Science or Andover. They know nothing about life. They know how to be poetic, but their poetry does not come out of suffering. They can turn out teachers of creative writing, not writers.

There was a student at Virginia who won a big fellowship, showed up for a month, and left. This money kept arriving each month, but there was no student to pick it up. Now *that's* a writer. We'll hear from him some day. That's a writer.

NB: Was the time you spent at the Iowa Writers' Workshop helpful to you?

JM: Yes. When I was there the camaraderie was good. The people in the department had energy and it was possible for the students to connect with that energy.

NB: *Did you learn anything about writing?*

JM: Sure. I had Richard Yates who's a practicing writer and he made useful suggestions, but I also think it's important and valuable to see a writer like Yates coping with life. The sense of reality that experience gives to the student is probably more valuable than technical devices picked up in the classroom.

NB: *Some people argue that exposure to writers with integrity helps students develop the kind of character you see in the student who walked out and left the fellowship money behind.*

JM: Character can't be taught. Your mother teaches you character; that's all that you're going to get. If you don't have a good mother, you won't have a good character. I had a good one. She told me, "Let them take your money—you can always get more of that —but don't let them take yourself."

N. SCOTT MOMADAY

*NB: I notice that you're in the comparative literature department.
Do you normally teach writing?*

SM: I prefer teaching literature courses; I don't teach writing very
often. I'm not comfortable about teaching creative writing because
I don't really believe that creative writing can be taught. Creative
writing courses—those I have taken as a student as well as those
which I have taught—tend to be courses in criticism. You can assign
a poem and then talk about things that are good and bad about it,
talk about alternative possibilities in this line or that. That's how I
have taught such courses and that's how courses that I've taken have
been taught, but I think students come into creative writing courses
wanting to come out of them able to write a poem or short story and,
as far as I can see, that's not how it works. Some people would
disagree with that, but they're probably people who are much better
at teaching creative writing than I am because they believe it's possible.

NB: Do you feel that any of your education helped your writing?

SM: You mean schooling?

NB: Yes.

SM: Not particularly. I think that was the least part of it. The
writing really came for me out of other kinds of education than the
schooling.

NB: Your Ph.D. was in English, wasn't it?

SM: Yes.

NB: I was interested in the comparison you draw between Tucker-man and Emerson in the introduction to your edition of Tuckerman. I understand you to be saying that Tuckerman was more sophisticated than Emerson because he could look at things scientifically as well as intuitively.

SM: That's certainly true. I don't know that "sophistication" is the word there, but he certainly knew more than Emerson did about science. Tuckerman's three great loves were poetry, botany and as-tronomy, perhaps in that order and his knowledge of botany and astronomy greatly informs his poems. Emerson didn't have that particular interest or knowledge and I think Tuckerman is a more responsible, a more effective, a more successful observer of nature for those reasons.

NB: Some people suggest that getting a Ph.D. is antithetical to writ-ing creatively.

SM: I don't think it's antithetical, but I don't think it has anything to do with it either. Writers don't need to have Ph.D.'s, but having one doesn't necessarily impede your writing.

NB: Were you able to write your own things when you were working on a doctorate?

SM: Yes, I came to Stanford as a creative writing student, so I was given time to write and money on which to live and good instruction. I took a course under Yvor Winters called, "The Writing of Poetry" several times. I learned a lot from Winters about the traditional forms of English poetry. I didn't learn how to write, but I learned how to recognize the structure of poetry and I could, with that learning, craft my writing in a way that I didn't know how to craft it before; and I found that useful. All the time I was at Stanford, I wrote poetry. Then when I left, I started writing other things too.

NB: Even though you don't teach creative writing often, some of the remarks you've made, not about writing, but about other things, sound like comments people who do teach creative writing have made about the writing process.

SM: For example . . .

NB: Well, the story about your father and his friend getting together to paint.

SM: From *The Names,* is that? Yeah, I remember—Quincy Tahoma.

NB: That episode struck me because it was so full of elation; there were a couple of things about it. One is that they work together. A justification for writing workshops is that it's hard to go off and write poems by yourself and feel that you're doing something that has a point.

SM: There's a basic distinction to be made there. You can sit at a painter's feet while he's working at the easel and you can, by observation, learn a good deal about what he does; but I don't think that applies to someone sitting at a typewriter. *(Laughter.)* I paint and I have spent very valuable time with Leonard Baskin, for example, watching him draw; I learned a lot from that. And I would love just to be in the same room with Fritz Scholder while he was painting because I'm sure I would learn a lot just by watching. But I don't think I could learn anything about writing by observing John Cheever sitting at a typewriter. You see the distinction I'm making?

NB: Sure.

SM: I think it's a valid one.

NB: Sure. But they were saying that if you're part of a writing community, you feel that wanting to write a story or wanting to write a poem is not a totally bizarre thing.

SM: Yes, it is. *(Laughter.)* Writing a poem is a bizarre thing. It's a brash and artificial act. I think it takes a peculiar sort of person to write a poem; there's a compulsion involved and a very creative one. I think you either have that need to express yourself in that way or you don't.

Maybe my temperament sets me apart from a good many other writers. I've never found any benefit in workshops or in communities of writers. When I came to Stanford as a creative writing fellow in poetry, I worked with other poets and we all wrote poems and exchanged them and talked about them. I don't think that was especially valuable to me, and I didn't have the sense at the time that this is how to do it. I think of writing as a very isolated business, a personal matter. When I was a student at Stanford, I was offered a fellowship at the Iowa Workshop, and Paul Engle was in charge of that program at the time. "We have a community of writers here and you will be able to exchange ideas," he said. The whole idea was that one writer stimulates another. That didn't appeal to me at all. In fact, it turned me off completely. I thought, "My good Lord, if I got myself into that sort of situation, I'd probably freeze instead of being productive." But I do understand that a lot of people feel differently about it. I guess it finally boils down to what enables *you* as a person to write and I find the best situation for my writing is isolation.

NB: There's another thing I wanted to ask you about that story: do you see any connection between the process of making things and the elation that you all experienced?

SM: Oh yes. *That* certainly would apply to writing too. There is an elation in it. There's a wide range of possibilities. And at the two extremes you have, on the one hand, complete frustration; that's when you sit down at the typewriter, and this has happened to me thousands, tens of thousands of times, you sit down with a good stretch of time in front of you, say a morning, and you have the best of intentions and nothing happens. You sit there for four hours and you have nothing to show for it. There are few frustrations greater than that. But if, on the other hand, at the other end of the spectrum, you sit down and after four hours you have a paragraph or two, maybe, or three, and you understand that you have done something well—there are few satisfactions greater than that. And I would talk about that in terms of elation, euphoria; you feel the way we did when my father and Quincy Tahoma and I went up into the mountains after one of those sessions. It was a great release, a great sense of having done well on their part; but it was so electric and contagious that I could share in that feeling, too. It was wonderful.

NB: Many people talk of trying to get their students to do what you did when you got on that horse in The Names *and said, "Let me hold to the way and be thoughtful in my going." You said that if you were going to enjoy that day thoroughly, you had just to let it happen. And that's an attitude people often identify as important to writing well. Does that make any sense to you?*

SM: The spontaneity?

NB: Yes.

SM: It does. I think that would apply to all teaching, regardless of the subject. There are always moments that come unexpectedly; they're always the best moments. Some one of your students who's said nothing for three weeks suddenly makes a brilliant observation, and that's thrilling. That kind of spontaneity would apply to writing as well. Someone writes something that takes you by surprise, and that's thrilling. It happens often enough to sustain your spirit.

NB: They also say that the writer has to cultivate an ability to be open to those things which come up spontaneously.

SM: Of course. Yes, yes. You never know what's going to happen. You never know what you're going to come up with at the end of an hour of writing; at least, I don't. I don't plan it ahead of time; I don't set a goal for myself and then reach it or not so much as I work and invest myself in the work without thinking of a specific goal. And then, after a time, if there's something there, it is bound to be surprising.

NB: Do you still write a newspaper column?

SM: Oh no. I wrote a column for the *Santa Fe New Mexican* for two years only. But it was fun. In a way, I'd like to do it again.

NB: Why did you do it in the first place?

SM: I'd always been interested in newspaper writing and I admired some columnists and so I made an inquiry at the *New Mexican.* They took me on and I had a wonderful time writing columns once a week over two years.

NB: What was the difference between doing that and the other kinds of writing you do?

SM: I didn't think of those columns as serious writing; they were exercises. And I was able to write on anything I wanted to, so it was fun. It was a kind of relaxation really.

NB: Did it interfere with your other writing?

SM: Not that I could see.

NB: What about teaching? Does it interfere with your writing?

SM: I don't think that teaching has ever taken up my writing time. When I was writing *The Names,* for example, I was working, at the most, five hours a day. I can't write more than that a day; that's the energy that I have to give to it. In my teaching, I've always kept my mornings free for writing and I couldn't use more time than that anyway. So, I don't think teaching has cut into my time for writing at all.

NB: Do you think that what you're teaching makes any difference to your writing?

SM: I haven't thought about that, but it probably does. If I'm teaching books that I admire very much, it probably is an incentive. I'm constantly coming upon passages in books that, no matter how many times I've read them, impress me in a new way and I feel a kind of inspiration: "Ah, that's well done. I could do that. I might just do something like that." It happens all the time.

The intellectual encounter is probably helpful too. You trade ideas with students; you are forced to articulate your ideas. I suppose in all that, there is some benefit to your writing. Better, say, than not to trade ideas with someone, not to be forced to articulate your ideas to a class. So teaching is probably beneficial in a great many different ways, not all of which I recognize.

NB: Do you have any particular goals for the students?

SM: Yes, each course has its own goals and objectives, but in general I want them not only to learn something, but to perform to their capacities. I look for excellence and if I don't get it, I'm disappointed and I grade the papers accordingly.

NB: What kinds of literature courses do you teach?

SM: I teach a course called, "The Autobiographical Narrative" which is an investigation of the first person voice and the viewpoint of the writer who is looking inward on his own experience and writing about it.

NB: That sounds like something you've done.

SM: *The Names* is an example of that particular form and I was very much interested in books of that kind when I was writing *The Names,* so I fashioned a course out of it. We read things like *Out of Africa, Speak, Memory* and *Goodbye to All That* and Sartre's *The Words* and Lillian Hellman's *Pentimento.* I'm teaching that course this quarter and for the first time I'm using a book called *This House of Sky* by Ivan Doig about growing up in Montana. It's wonderful. Regularly I teach a course in oral tradition which is focused on

American Indian oral tradition. And I teach a course called "Literature of the American West from 1850 to the Present," a course on the landscape in American Literature and a course on Emily Dickinson and Frederick Tuckerman.

NB: Your courses sound wonderful.

SM: They're fun. Yeah. I enjoy them.

NB: I imagine that you designed most of them.

SM: All of those I mentioned.

NB: Which comes first, the reading for the course or your own writing?

SM: It works both ways. I guess I had the idea of writing *The Names* before I had the idea of offering a course in the autobiographical narrative, so the course probably proceeded from my interest in writing in that form. But I'm sure it works the other way too. Every year you're sent a questionnaire as to what you propose to offer in the next year and that's the time when you think, "Ah, what might be fascinating to explore? What will the students find fascinating?" And so you are encouraged to be inventive.

NB: One thing that interested me in your writing was the idea that people are losing their sensitivity to words. Do you deal with that in your course on oral tradition?

SM: We talk a great deal about that in that course. It really is a fundamental examination of the way we exist in the element of language. It turns out to be a comparison between the oral tradition and the written tradition. It's great fun because few people think about their existence in language at that fundamental level. So it's fascinating and I learn a great deal every time I teach it. I think the students do too because I'm sure most of them have never thought about language in the way that I force them to think about it in that course. And we do, as you say, spend time talking about what words are and what their potential is for us in literature and in conversation —in every way.

When I first offered the course, I had no idea how it would be received. I was hoping that I could get maybe ten or twelve students together around a table. Well, 150 students showed up for the first meeting. I didn't want to turn anybody away, so I had to adjust my

idea of the course and it became a lecture course, which is not what
it should be; but so many people are interested in the subject that I've
had to give it as a lecture course most of the time. Every two years
or so, I allow myself the luxury of limiting enrollment to twenty and
then I call it by another name, "The Storyteller and His Art." And
we do sit around a table and we tell stories and we talk about what
the role of the storyteller is, how he exists in the language. It's never
the same thing twice; it's determined by the people in it. I've been
fortunate in having students who really wanted to participate, who
wanted to tell stories. I've given them the option at the end of the
course of either writing a paper or making an oral presentation and
a good number always opt for the oral presentation, and they've been
extremely imaginative and inventive: there have been stories, people
have put on skits, dueled each other at the level of language and done
other wonderful things. I try to simulate an oral situation; I try to
make them believe that they exist outside the written tradition and,
of course, they cannot do that. Nor can I. But to the extent that you
can make the attempt, it is valuable.

NB: Why?

SM: Because the understanding of language within the oral tradition is much more intense. It's a much more valid understanding of
language. Writing separates man from language one more degree;
writing creates a false security where language is concerned. But the
man who understands that he must pass whatever it is he has to
contribute to the next generation by word of mouth takes what he
says more seriously: he's more careful of what he says; he's less
wasteful of language; he relies to a much greater extent upon his
memory; he relies to a much greater extent upon his hearing. All of
this is what we try to understand about the oral tradition and it's
difficult. It requires a great act of the imagination and to the extent
that I can get my students to *want* and to *try* to make that act, it's
all to the good.

*NB: How can they pretend they're in an oral tradition? Are there
specific things you do, like forbid them to take notes?*

SM: That's right; that's right. I don't allow them to take notes and
there are no texts when I teach the story-telling part. Sometimes I
use texts as a springboard. We'll look at stories by Borges, for exam-

ple, who is a very imaginative writer, or we'll use *Seven Gothic Tales* or some of Chekhov's stories, maybe, just at the beginning so we can talk about what a story is and what the storyteller tries to do and what his relationship to the reader is. And then from there, we do away with all the printed materials and we tell stories and talk about the storyteller instead of the writer and the listener instead of the reader and make that crossing over from one tradition to the other. In some ways, it's futile because I don't think you can make the transition entirely, but you can at least suggest it and point to possibilities and I think that's extremely valuable. It has been for me personally and if it has been for me, then I think it ought to be for students too.

NB: How has it been valuable for you?

SM: I think by virtue of having looked as long as I have into oral tradition, I have a much keener appreciation of language than I would otherwise have. And I think that must show through in my writing. I hope so.

NB: A number of people who teach writing have mentioned that it is important for their students to read their work out loud in class, hear what they're writing.

SM: I would certainly agree with that. I tell all of my students, in literature courses as well as writing courses, that it's important to hear what you write. And when I'm composing, I babble to myself a lot. I speak it aloud to myself and I know by the sound of it whether it's what I want or not. It's one of my criteria for evaluating my writing. I must hear it.

NB: Your background probably has a lot to do with your consciousness of language. Has it been valuable to you in other ways?

SM: I grew up in a very rich and exotic world and I find myself constantly recalling things from that world. I loved it and I've written a good deal about it.

LISEL MUELLER

NB: How has being bilingual influenced your consciousness of language?

LM: We learn language by imitation; even people who don't know the grammar of their own language will speak it correctly if they hear it spoken correctly. Usage is another thing we just pick up. We don't think about our native language at all. But when you switch to another language, you are conscious of *everything*. You're conscious of the grammatical constructions, you're conscious of the phrasing, you're conscious of the idioms, you're conscious of each word—what it means, how it is used in its various forms, its derivation, if there is a cognate in your own language, how it might differ—all those things become so important. And metaphor is difficult at first. Like the popular song "Under a blanket of blue": I knew from the context it couldn't be a real blanket, but I didn't know it was the sky. And I didn't know "deep purple" meant nightfall. In German, I would have understood, any American would have understood . . . except we don't really listen to the words of popular songs in our native language. We hear those words, we say those words, and we never think about what they mean or whether they make any sense. I didn't in Germany, but coming here it became extremely important to be able to understand what every word meant. It's that kind of minute attention I think you have only with a language to which you're not native. Who knows, I might not have become a poet had this not happened to me.

My poetry is largely Germanic in the sense that I usually use strong, short words and not many latinates because they sound

96

weaker to me—conversational, essayistic. More and more latinates are coming into poetry because our whole speech is becoming more latinate. The younger people use words ending in -ion and so on much more freely than I would. Of course, that isn't unique to me. Look at Dylan Thomas or Hopkins or Roethke who almost exclusively used Germanic words, probably because they dealt with very elementary things. My poems too tend to deal with the elementary and I associate those strongly accented, strongly sounded Germanic words with elementary things. If you're going to discuss ideas, then latinates are appropriate; but I don't deal with them, at least not directly, in my poems.

NB: A number of people have commented that a fascination with language rather than an interest in ideas is the primary impetus for writing poetry.

LM: There are very few ideas worth talking about. Those ideas are good for all times, but unless a poet has a new way of dealing with those ideas, they become commonplace. And new insights, new connections, are inseparable from their language, which is why a paraphrase of a poem always sounds banal.

NB: Your later poetry seems more concerned with political and moral issues than your earlier poetry, or am I imagining things?

LM: No, I think that's true and I think the Vietnam War changed me. That's when I became angry about what was going on. Those were bad years for me, not in terms of my private life, but in terms of being involved in the shame and guilt and wrongness of this country. Like many of us at that time, I took it all very personally, and perhaps the history of Nazi Germany in the back of my mind made me feel involved with it. Also, my father was a historian much involved with contemporary history and perhaps the genes started to take.

NB: I also thought you implied that the large ethical and political questions post-war German writers had to confront enriched their work.

LM: World War I destroyed a lot of the assumptions, but lip service was still given to the nineteenth century virtues and values of decency and humanity and honesty. All of these assumptions were *gone* after World War II. They had all proved to be illusions. It was like starting from scratch for the writers who survived. They had a lot to catch up on. For about twenty years they had been virtually cut off from new European and American writing. There was a total physical leveling of much of Germany and thousands starved to death even after the war was over. Then there were all the revelations about the death camps and the whole *monstrous history* which had occurred as a result of the Nazis in Germany. So it was like starting from scratch both physically and spiritually. And it was important to find a new, untainted language. This is why a lot of the poetry seems very innovative as well as very stark—almost stammering to come up with something new. And the novelists had a whole new subject. The Germans have had to come to grips with their history and they get their strength from writing about it.

NB: Your poem "The Fall of the Muse" seems critical of American poetry.

LM: It was written against the exhibitionism I thought was going on, not just in poetry—although the confessional poets are implicated in this. It was written after the death not only of Sylvia Plath, but of Judy Garland and Marilyn Monroe and biographers on talk shows were trying to top each other with intimate details about these people's lives. I felt moral outrage about this public suffering and this *glamorizing* of suffering. The temptation is to keep upping the ante and finally all you're left with is committing suicide.

NB: I think that some contemporary American writers romanticize neurosis and I tend to avoid teaching their work, although that may be a mistake.

LM: For obvious historical reasons American writers tend to focus on private psychic suffering, rather than the suffering brought on by social and political injustice. That kind of suffering is no less real than the suffering of a brutalized oppressed person, but it's less shareable. We feel that someone who really has it *rough* in the world . . . we feel that kind of suffering is more justified somehow than the suffering that goes on in so much of the more privileged part of society.

I don't know which makes the better writing because some of the novels that have come out of the more realistic, proletarian writing of the thirties and so on, haven't stood up either.

There is a problem with finding subject matter in our society, partly because there is a great bias among young writers against political writing. They don't want to write about political matters at all. Robert Bly and Denise Levertov have been attacked for their engagement in these issues—the Vietnam War and nuclear disarmament and things of that sort. That seems to me a uniquely American and English tradition of disassociating writing from what goes on in the world because it's certainly not true of European writers and it's not true of South American writers. They're all involved in the politics of their country and they write about that; in countries where they can't write about it directly, like South Africa, Eastern Block countries, and Latin American countries, they write parables. They do it in an indirect way, but it's clearly understood.

NB: That certainly was a prejudice when I was in graduate school: bad writing is ideological and good writing is subtle and intricate. I used to think it was intellectual elitism: the best writing is the most inaccessible.

LM: A friend once gave a poetry reading and after the reading someone came up to him and said, "I enjoyed your poetry even though I can understand it." So, yes, there has been a lot of that. Luckily, I think that is changing.

NB: Some people have said that it's not good for literature to have so many writers sheltered by the academy.

LM: I don't know that it makes writing any less good, but I think it probably does make it more uniform. A lot of poets of our time sound very much alike; perhaps that's come out of the fact that most of us are teachers or writing students rather than working at Sears or driving a truck, or whatever. Writers used to have to support themselves in ways that had nothing to do with writing and this may make a difference in terms of struggling by yourself.

NB: You've written that you did exercises to teach yourself how to write poetry. Do you remember what they were?

LM: I did things like getting books on prosody out of the library and doing some of the things that were explained in there. For example, I would read about the villanelle and I would make myself write a villanelle. It was just a matter of reading books that explained the various forms and experimenting with them; I learned how they worked and tried to do some of them myself.

NB: Do you use anything like that with your students?

LM: It depends on the level of the students. Recently I've been teaching in a tutorial program and dealt largely with students who are already writers, graduate students. They know what they want to do and so I don't give them exercises. I let them write and then we discuss the work at hand. I suggest poets for them to read because I can see certain directions which I would like them to go in or certain things which I feel are not good about their work and I want them to read people they can learn from.

I've done some poetry in the schools and I give exercises with kids because you can't just say, "Sit down and write a poem." You have to give them specific instructions. Younger children are wonderful at metaphor. "Something is like something else" is a very simple way of explaining metaphor. "What does this remind you of?" "What is the color pink like for you?" Blue is an interesting color because some kids come up with all sad images and others come up with wonderful exhilarating blue images. Also, with natural phenomena, they're wonderful. I remember one kid saying, "Hail is like God dropping the ice cube out of his martini."

NB: Should I have my students read work they will understand even if it means they'll be reading Sandburg?

LM: It depends on the student. It depends on the age and the level you're talking about. If you're teaching graduate students, no. Or if you have some ambitious young intellectual who will want to read only things that he or she can't understand . . . But high school students, yes, Give them something they can enjoy because most of them don't like poetry to begin with, or think they won't like it, so give them work that can somehow touch on their own experience, that's simple enough and yet respectable poetry. Don't give them Rod McKuen, don't give them Edgar Guest, but . . . Sandburg may not be the greatest poet we've ever had, but he was a poet. You need to start with something you don't feel bad about giving them, but which will engage their interest.

You have to grab them where they are. Then you may be able to get them to go on from there, but if you give them something that shuts them out at the beginning, you'll never get them.

NB: I was interested by your poem about giving your daughter a copy of Sister Carrie *because a student once told me that the first time a book engrossed her was when we read* Sister Carrie *in class. The next term she got caught up in* The Grapes of Wrath, *but she thought the ending was too sad. I said, "Well, there's some hope that the Okies will get together." And she said, "Oh, I hope they do."*

LM: Well, that's it. For young people the personal connection is very important. "Oh, I hope they do," it's as if it were happening to her own family. I have noticed that often someone who has read one of my books, a young student or someone who has come to a reading of mine, will come up and tell me about a poem they have liked, and it's almost always, "I know someone who has done this" or "I have felt this way" or "I've had this experience." They don't respond to it because it's a well-written poem; it's because there's something in the poem that touches them personally. That's always the beginning; the aesthetic thing comes later.

I was reading Sandburg my first year in this country, when I wasn't used to the language. At the same time I was reading Sandburg, I was taking my first high school English Literature course. I was reading Wordsworth and Keats and Gray and I couldn't do much with them. They were simply too difficult for me; but Sandburg, I could read, I could understand, I could respond to. I knew that Keats and Wordsworth and Shelley and the rest were supposed to be much greater poets, but that didn't mean I really liked them.

NB: You've said that you wrote in free verse because you found "the echoes of the formal masters too strong" for your "incubating voice." Do your students have trouble with echoes?

LM: They have echoes, but they aren't those same echoes because they largely read contemporary poetry; so there'll be echoes of maybe Mark Strand or Galway Kinnell. It's never the traditionally formal poets because my students come from two generations in which they've not been taught metric poetry. A few years ago Donald Hall was teaching a short course in writing in iambic pentameter in the Goddard MFA Program, and students flocked to it. They found it extremely difficult and they found it fascinating: they were learning *new things.* And they found it very hard because they were used to speech rhythms; they were not used to hearing stressed and unstressed syllables. It was like learning to hear poetry in that way for the first time. So everything is turned around.

I've always, for example, liked to have my students read people like Richard Wilbur, who is an absolutely marvelous poet in whatever he does, but who, among other things, is very good with forms. And also someone like Marilyn Hacker who writes not only wonderful villanelles and sestinas and sonnets, but crowns of sonnets and double villanelles. She uses these very traditional forms, but uses extremely colloquial, idiomatic, contemporary language within these forms which I think is a beautiful and interesting combination. I like my students to read these people. It doesn't necessarily mean they write like them. It is hard for them to, say, write a sonnet that doesn't sound like tenth-rate Keats.

NB: If it's possible, I'd like you to explain this comment: "Once the tools, tricks and secrets of the trade become second nature, you lose the attention to technique which has served as a margin of safety. Suddenly you are nakedly exposed to the dangerous process of bringing a poem into existence."

LM: I meant that period between the time you know exactly what you do because you are doing an exercise and the time when you can trust your instinct and critical judgment enough that you don't feel totally at risk. It's like a child learning to walk. The child has held onto the furniture or the hands of grownups and then she lets go and for a little while, there'll be quite a few falls until, eventually, she stops falling and can walk by herself. There is a period like that and it's very troublesome for young writers. I certainly went through that for a number of years.

I get this in workshops where people who don't have much background in writing but a great deal of enthusiasm have no sense of whether the poem works and also whether it communicates its ideas to an outside reader. Often they're very good at criticizing poems by other people but they can't do it to their own poems. I'll talk to them about a specific poem and try to help them see some of the problems and they will say, "Well, you've been very helpful and now I see what you mean, but why can't I do this myself?" There's no way except the experience of writing and writing and revising, going back, looking at your old poems. There comes a day when you can do it, when the flaws jump out at you.

NB: It sounds as though that middle period is a time when the person hasn't really established a center for his or her work.

LM: That's true, but it's also a matter of learning the craft. Most young writers are very awkward in their language. Even if there's a great deal of talent there, a great deal of energy, the phrasing is usually not smooth yet, not lapidary enough. It's also proportion and pace and transition, how to get from here to there, all those technical things which you have to learn by feel on your own. You develop your own voice, your own language, and that takes time.

NB: Can having other people react to their work speed that process up?

LM: I think it can and that's why workshops are so valuable and such a shortcut for writers. It's something I didn't have when I started to write. Students in workshops get that immediate response from a teacher who's an experienced writer and from their fellow students.

NB: If someone couldn't go to a workshop, what would you suggest they do to teach themselves?

LM: Read the best poets—all the good poets of their time as well as the older literature. We learn to write by imitation largely, just as we learn to speak and walk by imitation. I think most teachers— probably all poets teaching—would agree that they're merely helping along and that the reading is the primary thing. The teacher can be very valuable in helping direct students to what to read. One of the good things about the Goddard program, now at Warren Wilson College, is that each program is individually made up for a particular student, and that it requires a lot of reading. It encourages not only reading poetry and criticism and fiction, but also reading outside of literature—reading about science or architecture or psychology— other subjects that could feed into your poetry as subject matter and enrich your sense of the world. Sometimes young writers don't want to read anything outside of literature and that's a very small part . . . The world is rich. Any writer is a better writer the less insulated he or she is.

Reading widely makes you a livelier, richer person and that would feed into your writing. It's probably more important for novelists than for poets because they deal with social reality whereas poets deal largely with their inner world or how their inner world relates to the outer world, but I think it enriches the whole *context* in which you write. W. H. Auden, for example, regretted very much that he didn't know more about nature, especially botany and zoology, than he did. He felt it would have helped his poetry a great deal if he had been able to use that area of knowledge in a natural way, the way, for example, Roethke did.

Even being a good writer, but *definitely* being a *great* writer, demands a great deal of understanding and knowledge of the world. It doesn't necessarily mean a formal education, but it does involve curiosity. That's what we feel in Tolstoy and Thomas Mann and Flaubert and the great poets like Yeats or Keats. One has that sense that they were interested in a very large universe.

I'm partial to history. To me a sense of what has gone on in the past is very important to one's view of the world. Because that is my bias in writing poetry, I look at what is going on right now in my life and the life of people around me not as divorced from everything that has gone before, but in the context of the past and of what may come in the future. Now that's not everyone's bias. For some people it may be nature. Everything related to the seasonal, to the rejuvenation of nature, or perhaps it relates to landscape. There are poets whose whole world of inner experience is articulated in terms of natural images; it's as if the landscape or the weather is a metaphor always for what is going on inside them. There are many different possibilities.

I don't mean a writer can't be a wonderful writer and have a highly concentrated vision. There are writers who are obsessed by one thing and that one thing is expressed over and over and wonderfully. It's the hedgehog and the fox idea. The hedgehog is the one who burrows inside; Kafka is a typical hedgehog. He had this one idiosyncratic vision of everything, and it was such a *powerful* vision . . . perhaps if he had dissipated it, it would not have been so powerful. And then there are the foxes like Tolstoy. But I think even for the obsessive ones, knowing as much as possible is valuable and a joy.

NB: Do you get anything from teaching?

LM: I've enjoyed the method of tutorial teaching very much. I like working with one person at a time, being able to relate to his or her particular needs, and see the direction they're going in. I can't really help someone without understanding their poetry [and that] means trying to get into that person's mind.

I like the exchange of talking about literature. Having to do it by mail, as I've had to with my students, is laborious, but it makes you think hard about everything you say because it's down on paper and there are so many more possibilities of misunderstanding. It's taught me to think about things more clearly than I would otherwise. It's also forced me to read a lot more because I've had to keep up with the students' reading and they want to read a lot of things I haven't read. It's been stimulating for me. There is the pleasure of the intellectual-literary exchange, but also of seeing someone develop and maybe having a share in guiding their development.

WILLIAM STAFFORD

WS: Let's say only good things now.

NB: *All right—only very intelligent things.*

WS: All right, I'll do my best.

NB: *When you talk about writing poetry, you usually talk about letting things happen.*

WS: It's a strong impulse of mine to put that into any such conversation about writing because I feel that it's important to let the process of writing bring about things rather than be just the writing down of things that are already brought about. Some people talk about writing as if it's penmanship: you take dictation from your psyche that has already done something. Well, I'm interested in the psyche that hasn't done something and then does something. What does it do in between? So I always try to get the people to relax enough to pay attention to the things that actually occur to them during the process of writing. Does this make any sense?

NB: *That makes sense, but how do you do it?*

WS: I do it in any way I can keep them from feeling that they have to be on guard about what they write or that they have to have it all formulated before they begin or that there are unallowable things in dignified discourse. I'd like to go all out on this and confront as squarely as possible those who make students feel that writing is something that is done with the fully conscious, already accomplished self. I think writing is itself educational, exploratory, and worthy of trust while you're doing it. So if you think of something while you're writing, that's fine.

I still feel the weight of your question, "How do you get them to do that?" It's partly by creating an atmosphere of trust in the classroom. It's partly by joining them in whatever reactions we have: they sometimes feel funny about what they write, so I feel funny about it too, but I don't inhibit it. Well, there is one other thing I'd put in somewhere; I might as well put it in now: I think approval of student writers is scary to writers. I keep meeting teachers who say, "Oh, yes. I'm very nice to the students. I always find something to praise." I don't like that. I would rather be in neutral or the way I would be with a friend discussing something that neither of us has a fixed position on but which we are both exploring so that the friend or the student doesn't feel that they have to get that approval by doing something good again. That just extends the area of inhibition.

NB: Oh, because they learn to write for the approval.

WS: That's right.

NB: Rather than for themselves.

WS: Yes. It has the same effect as criticism, really, because even approval is the implied presence of possible criticism. So there's someone you give a lot of approval to, everybody else gets it from the other end, "They got it. Now how can I get it?" I don't see any way around that. I don't know why I have so much trouble with teachers about it.

NB: So you just discuss what they've written and . . .

WS: Yeah and I would like our discourse to be about those things that don't have to do with praise or blame but have to do with more or less, or "Did you do it like this? Tell me more about why you did it like this," and not the automatic stance that is almost always imposed upon teachers of being the evaluator. I'm not evaluator; I'm participant.

NB: Are you able to get away without grading them?

WS: I have been able to get away without putting grades on the papers; this is a little bit different from not grading at all. Many places where I've taught, I did have to grade the students at the end of the term; but I would try to separate that function from the teaching function. The teaching part I would keep as far as possible from reminding them that they are in this area where there are mine fields they have to cross in which they might ruin their grade. So as much as possible, I would postpone, dilute, avoid, play down the idea of evaluation. They would, I suppose, always know that sooner or later I'd have to grade them. But that's not part of our daily life; that's not part of the learning. That's part of what the society has imposed upon us in this institution. That's what I tell them. I think the grading procedure endangers creativity. This isn't entirely easy on them because they've gotten used to being evaluated.

NB: Oh sure, or being told how to do it; that's much more comforting.

WS: Either told how to do it or praised. Some people have said, "Well, Bill, you're so soft-hearted." No, No, it isn't that. It's more scary than that. But it's not scary in the sense of being haunted throughout the process of writing by the need to tailor-make what you're doing for the approval of the teacher.

NB: Is there anything else you do?

WS: Yes, a whole lot of things. One is I try to induce in the classroom an atmosphere in which it is possible for reactions to come from all directions, not just from me. I've done it many ways. I have a box in which I put all their papers and say, "Here are the papers for this class. Take a look. Read it." And they either read it in their room or check it in at the reserved book desk; so when we talk about a paper in a class, there are many reactions. But they're the kind of reactions that come straight across at the writers, not from high down to the writer, straight across from the peers. And once that atmosphere is established in the room, I can even hazard a remark myself now and then. But mostly I don't, especially early. I learned if I start the term by being either the one who does the evaluating or, and this is even more insidious with the same effect, the one who summarizes the discussion at the end, I'm still doing it; so I don't want to be the terminal remarker on a paper. I would rather have a paper slip through with *horrendous* things in it than spoil the system of the class by saying, "The rest of you have failed to notice that . . . " or "Let me summarize what's been said here," and then sort of correct everyone. Oh no. Once I can enter in like a peer, which I really am, but the system has not admitted that, then I try to do it.

There are many other quirks because the atmosphere in the classroom is induced by many little things: body language, where I sit, the time I get to class, whether I have a list of things we have to do —all sorts of things. And I just kind of weasel in on the class, sit in on the class, don't have any announcements about tests, or anything like that.

NB: You teach creative writing, but you have also taught composition and literature.

WS: I would apply this to all kinds of writing. And talk, as a matter of fact. So all the teaching for me was a term-long finessing encounter with a room full of people who were to be wooed over into telling me what they knew and what they didn't know and the extent to which they knew it and the extent to which they didn't know it. And I had to go past some obstacles that had been trained into them.

NB: A lot of obstacles.

WS: A lot of obstacles. You know, I got a long-distance look and I feel you did too because we're thinking about those times in class in which . . . Well, the ideal I thought of was the time when there's someone who hasn't done well in school who hands in a paper and you know it wouldn't pass one of those other courses, and you don't either praise this person for that paper or blame this person for that paper, but suddenly you're just in it together and your eyes meet and you look at certain things and those things that they are ready to have some slight adjustment to, they do half the adjusting and you do the other half. This is where I'd like to get. I don't want to be at a height, or holding them up, but just sort of looks of recognition between us. And if you get it right, it hardly makes any difference what you say. You can say, "It's terrible, isn't it?" It's OK, for they know it's terrible in the area where we're all terrible.

NB: Did your teaching interfere with your writing at all?

WS: Well, I sometimes thought wistfully about those who didn't have to do any work at all. But if I was going to have to work, I didn't feel menaced by teaching, partly because of the point of view I had about writing, that I wasn't learning techniques that were going to turn me into automation as a writer, that I was continuously learning from this lowest person in the class as well as from others. They had all sorts of ideas and I could roll my eyes as much with them as with anybody. So that's what I'm looking for, that ongoing encounter, and I thought teaching was always full of richness. Any job that tired you out so much or discouraged you so much or dulled you so much would be a hazard to other activity. But I don't quite understand how teaching in which you have all these level encounters about books, about ideas, all these lively people, I don't see why it's a menace to associate with lively people. If you get tired of lively people, I suppose you do sometimes, well, you can always go home and I often did. My dog would be duller.

NB: I notice that you've had other kinds of jobs and I wonder if any of them were particularly useful or not useful to your writing?

WS: This is sort of the obverse of the other: is teaching a hazard? Well, I say I don't know why it would be hazard. So I turn to the other jobs and think, "Are they a special help?" Oh no, they're sort of like teaching. I remember all the conversations when I worked in the oil refinery and lots of lively people there. And forest service; I liked that. And sugar beet fields; it had its own kind of heroism. Stoop crops are front line productive activity; it's sort of fun to do that: survive the sun, be able to make a living at something that hard. There were many others too, like construction work and electrician's helper and things like that; I would have done more things too, if I'd had the chance. The jobs are full of encounters, people; even the dead periods, hoeing weeds around the oil tank—that's a nice, repetitive, vistas-over-your-shoulder kind of job.

NB: Was any part of your education especially helpful to your writing? Were there any particularly valuable times, like the time you spent at Iowa? Or was it all a continuum?

WS: My general reaction to school was good. All the way through I had all sorts of wonderful adventures. School was a good place. They had more books at school than we had at home, that makes it nice; magazines, interesting people, all sorts of good projects for us to do and I always had a lot of gusto for school. But that forces me to respond to your other question, "Were there certain times . . . Was the time at Iowa crucial?" I don't mean to demean Iowa by saying, "No, that was not crucial": for one thing, I went there pretty late in my writing; for another, I don't think any one time is crucial.

I think the lucky way, the way I prefer, is a generally positive succession of enounters. And I feel that I had them: many of my teachers, many books that came my way, whole spells of reading. I smack my lips when I think of how good it was. So there are just a lot of good books; that's one thing. And you find them some places and not others. And I've always liked libraries and schools and people who were engaged in libraries and schools. Garden City Junior College: excellent! El Dorado Junior College: wonderful! University of Kansas: really great! Iowa: I loved it!

NB: Once when you were talking about what "allegiances" means, you said, "It's like assuming good will on the part of people—I tend to do that. It's like a kind of level look at every day's experiences as it comes at you and welcoming it. I feel that." When I read something like that, I see a connection between your point of view and the way you write poetry. For you, the process of writing poetry is a process of accepting and it seems to me that could easily become extended to other things.

WS: I think what I'm trying to locate is that condition of a being who has not been distorted from the receptive, accurate encounter with experience. It's possible to overlearn fear or overlearn confidence. The conditions of life are such that make survival depend on the organism's ability to come back level again and be ready for the conditions of life as they are on the earth. There are people who are oversensitized. The intellectual position is to be a good—let me see, what am I after, what instrument shall I use? What they use to measure earthquakes: seismograph. An individual's intellect and emotions should be like a good seismograph: sensitive enough to register what happens, but strong enough not to be wrecked by the first little thing that happens. And so human beings have to occupy that position between being so steady and dumb and dull that they can't register and being so sensitive that they're wrecked by anything they register. So I just try to get into the readiness and be receptive, not stampeded, not overly trustful. I suppose we're all looking for that, but I feel the formulations that some people use disguise the necessity for avoiding both extremes. It's very easy to make powerful poems out of suffering all the time. It's all right; but that makes you a casualty.

NB: What did you mean when you said, "So I try not to learn, disengage, because reasons block the next needed feelings"?

WS: It links partly to this idea that for some people writing is done by fully preparing the being to come out with nothing but totally worthy utterances. And the only way to do that is not to step off the path. You've got to step off the path if you're going to explore new places; so I don't want to learn so well that I'm not learning from the encounter of now with the language. And if I had a wish to express at this point, it would be, "Save me from actually having or assuming I have the fully trained ability to write whatever is assigned to me." The person who assigned it may not have seen something that a more stupid person would enable them to see. You could both be programmed so well that nothing would ever happen to you but around and around. And that is what does happen to some writers: around and around. It's the equivalent of officialese in encounters; you get a clear, well worked-out and often totally irrelevant response.

NB: In another interview, someone said that "contemporary poets often seem to be super-neurotics in a neurotic world," and you said, "You shouldn't have neuroses. You ought to be on the level."

WS: *(Laughter.)* Well . . .

NB: I'm very confused about where the cliché that artists are neurotic comes from. It seems to me that doing the kinds of things you're talking about takes a lot of courage. As you said, it's scary for your students to let go of patterns and virtually everyone I've interviewed says that's central to writing well.

WS: Analyzing someone who does something unusual, maybe people need to have locutions to use, so they say writers are neurotic. They operate in a different way from a carpenter, but carpenters are neurotic, of course, as everybody knows. In fact, when I was getting ready to put windows in our house, the glass person said, "We people who work with glass are really neurotic." *(Laughter.)* He said, "You'd better not try to do that glass yourself. You'll find out why." Well, I'll put it this way, in a positive way: I'm willing to take all sorts of tentative classifications about what we're like, we writers, but there's something I'd like to cling to and that is the essential thing that we're doing. And the essential thing we're doing is we're having enough faith in our own perceptions and decisions to make them paramount. You've just got to do it, if you're an artist. So you can say it's arrogance, or you can say it's neurotic, you can say it's humility in the face of the pattern the words want to take, you can have all sorts of myths about it; I don't care what myth you have, you've got to make the decisions yourself, if you're an artist. And I would like to have students realize that as soon as possible. They come into class and the first thing they want to say to me: "How am I doing?" "What do you think?" is the rejoinder, with body language, or raised eyebrows, evasion . . . .

NB: Once you said, "It would be too much to claim that art, the practice of it, will establish a 'good,' a serene, a superior self. No. But art will, if pursued for itself, bring into sustained realization the self most centrally yours, freed from its distortions, brought from greed or fear or ambition."

WS: I remember that.

NB: I don't quite understand the distinction you're making because a self that is more centrally yours and freed from greed, fear, or ambition, sounds pretty good to me.

WS: I probably ought to tone that down a bit, but I forgive myself for saying that partly because I was coming out on that skate from avoiding the other skate. The early part of that is I didn't want to claim that one should assume that one is creating something worthy of the ages. Not at all. So the product is expendable, but the process is precious. This is what I'd like to say. I keep meeting poets who say something like, "Well, I'm going to try to do something that is worthy and lasting and beyond my lifetime and so on." I think that's just frivolous. That's something only society decides and I don't see that it makes any difference anyway. But the process is the process of living centrally and paying attention to your own life. Surely that's worth doing. If you don't, who will? That's what living is about and you can be distracted from living by trying to create things that will last in the terminology and the mode of society that may or may not be harmonious to your life. So I want to shrug that part off.

I think it is a big claim and if it hadn't been an interview, probably, if I had been carefully phrasing it, I would have tried to accomplish the same thing without making such forensic claims for art. I don't want to make claims for it, but I'd like to recognize what I think I see in it and that is a real art, genuine art, comes not from hammering out something for posterity, but from making the discoveries that are yours to be made because of your unique constitution and the unique encounter you have in experience.

NB: Are there ever any days you don't write?

WS: There are no days I can't write.

NB: Are there ever any days you don't write?

WS: There are days I don't write. For instance, I'm headlong from somewhere to somewhere else and full of distractions, and I forgive myself for those days; it's not a fetish, I think, but most days I do write.

NB: Does that change the day at all?

WS: Yes. It changes the day a little bit. For me, for analogy, it's sort of like jogging. If I've done my jogging, it's an OK day. If I've done my writing, it's a really OK day. It's a confirming, satisfying activity to do. And it's almost devotional. Maybe that's too strong, but it's as if a day of my life deserves a little attention from my life. It's my kind of attention to stop long enough, to let the evaluative, the speculative, the exploratory impulses that are native to that portion of my time be manifest in a sustained way so that I can recognize them and get sustenance from them.

NB: One person I talked to said that you're a totally natural poet and another said that everything you write is poetry.

WS: Is that right? *(Laughter.)*

NB: And I wonder how you got that way?

WS: Well, "How I got those words" is the way I'd phrase it. I think that these people you talked to were generous people and I don't lightly dismiss their words. I take seriously what they said, so I try to figure out, "Now, what does this mean?" I think they're locating a kind of writing that grows out of my perception of what writing is, so I'd like to say a little bit about that.

Poems and stories and helpfully enhanced discourse of any kind, I think, are results of a trustful, undistorted entry into the language that's natural to yourself. And I suddenly glimpse the possibility of conceptualizing language as something that can be exactly congruent with your mental life. That congruency is menaced by many things: competitiveness, systematic educational distortion toward prizes, maybe even being bullied by those around you so that you just don't have the bounce that it takes to get into your thought and language. And so I hark back to something and that is, in our home, our parents were receptive to what we said. I never felt it necessary to distort my language or even in any serious way disguise my plans. Maybe my mother didn't want me to go fishing on Cow Creek, but we knew we were both operating in an area of general acceptance. And I think maybe that's important. So I hark back to the way I'd like to have a classroom so people can let that congruency between thought and language have its way with their discourse. I think as human beings, insofar as we cherish each other, we cherish that trust that it's all right to live your own life and even to have your own thoughts and occasionally in a mild voice to express them.

NB: Someone asked you when you found out you were a poet and you said that you wondered more about when everyone else stopped.

WS: Yes, yes. The kind of process we are talking about is native to everyone, kids with their hopscotch and so on. Everyone. Everyone I've ever met, everyone, has what to me is the essential element of what we're talking about. They may not write what they call poems, but they make remarks they like better than other remarks. They have that lipsmacking realization of differences in discourse. But then later they may feel, "I'm a salesman. I'm not allowed to have any lipsmacking impulses about things. I'm going to give it the way it is in the book." And so they quit, as far as I'm concerned, at least that part of their lives. So I don't think it was just a cute way to keep from saying a time, although it is hard to say a time for me; I don't know a time when I wasn't enjoying language. And I guess that's what a poet does. But I think everyone shares in this and it's artificial to think there's a life without it. They're asking the question from the point of view that poetry is something that you have to nerve yourself to do. I don't think that's true. Not to do poetry is possible, I suppose, but it's hard and I never met anyone who didn't do it in some sense of coursing sounds, of being either delighted or discouraged about how the sentence comes out, by responding or not responding to what somebody says. You're really in a tough spot if you don't have any of those responses. And so they're asking me to enter a universe in which the values I hold dear are reversed when they ask that question. I just don't want to go into that world, so I stop.

NB: *How do you feel about workshops and the fact that there are more and more poets all the time?*

WS: I feel all right about workshops. And I don't know what they mean about more and more poets all the time. Maybe there are. In fact, I think, maybe there are; but what's this viewing-with-alarm bit? I feel that this process that's so rewarding is a right for everybody. And for those who teach workshops thinking that they are going to sift out a few gifted individuals and turn them into Miltons and Shakespeares and that the presence of other people is a problem for Miltons and Shakespeares, I say they've got it wrong. *(Laughter.)* Maybe I shouldn't elaborate, but I feel strongly about that. I feel that that point of view about the desirability of only a limited number and those only of the elite engaged in an activity as rewarding as poetry is almost like treason of the intellectual realm or the cultural realm. I'll do it the positive way by saying, if I go to a class, I feel I'm meeting a succession of people to whom I owe individually total allegiance and succession. I'm not looking for the ones who are going to enhance the school or my reputation or their own. That's nice, but as a teacher I believe that if there is such a thing as the lowest one in the class, they deserve the same level reception and cordiality as anybody else.

NB: *Are you saying something about schools in your poem "Accountability"?*

WS: Yes, I am saying things about schools. I dream my way back into it now. I was in Wyoming, in a boom town, Gillette. We were welcomed by the teachers and the students in this town. The high school is on a hill above the town; it's a boom town with trailers and quick constructions and no perspective down the road except another boom town. I'm not trying to indict Gillette or any other town; it's just that high school students are inducted into the hall of high school with lockers, with limited library, with military recruitment posters. I saw another one this afternoon in the high school where

I was right here in Michigan. I was looking for a magazine and all I could find was military recruitment posters and those were free and you had access to them, but the magazines you had to write out a big thing. Well, it's that sort of thing that I felt in the school. I suppose it's forced on us and so I'm not trying to indict anyone, but I suddenly felt forlorn. I thought those who talk about accountability in schools think they're talking about split infinitives or something —trivialities. I'm talking about lives, vision, hope, something plain like kindness and humility and they'd throw their kids into a school that would teach them all about split infinitives and send them straight over to drop atom bombs on someone. Is that accountability?

WALLACE STEGNER

NB: What was your goal when you taught writing?

WS: If you aren't a person, if you're only a copy of a person, you aren't going to write very well. And most people who come to university writing programs are gifted; they're people, or potential people. The ideal is to give them every possibility to realize their potential in their own particular way—not by way of imitation.

NB: How do you do that?

WS: It's a difficult, slippery, socratic business. You can't assert your own beliefs too strongly because people are impressionable. Whenever I was teaching writing, I let them go in their own way, even when I felt they were failing, because I didn't want to stir up a bunch of little carbon copies of myself. On the other hand, a lot of wind and nonsense goes on in the head of a young writer just finding out what he wants to write about and who he is. That has to be laughed away without destroying his enthusiasm. It's not a teacher's function to turn people on; if they aren't self-starters, they don't belong there. It *is* a teacher's function to avoid turning them off; it's an easy racket to get discouraged in. So you work differently with different people. Some students you couldn't discourage with an ax and some students—not necessarily the worst ones—discourage very easily. The teacher's job is to keep them writing, keep them enthusiastic about what they're doing, and keep them believing in what they're doing. When someone has no proof that he *can* write, it's easy for him to feel that this is not the way to spend his life. So you abrade rather than abuse the work students offer.

NB: *Did you conduct workshops, distribute copies, and so on?*

WS: More and more, in later years, I had people read their own stories. If they were too shy to read them, I read them because reading aloud enforces a kind of attention that reading silently does not, and it gives the victim a much greater sense of how his stuff sounds to somebody else. Any piece of writing reveals its excrescences a bit more plainly when read aloud. It may be even better to have somebody else read it aloud to the author because then he's not worrying about the impression he's making; he's listening to what he wrote. It takes time, but it does more for the manuscript and for the writer of the manuscript than other methods I've tried. Prose ought to be written for the ear as well as the eye. You've got to hear it. I'm enough of a spoiled poet to think that if it doesn't have cadences, somehow, it isn't prose. There are good books that are bad prose, but I wouldn't want to write them.

NB: *Do you encourage students to make a habit of reading their work aloud?*

WS: Oh, sure. And to read at large. If you're not a hungry reader, you're not likely to be a writer. Reading is one way you learn writing. You learn it through the pores, often without knowing you're learning it. People who have read a lot are likely to have some kind of reasonable style and some notion of how to tell a story and some notion of form without ever having thought about those things.

NB: *You've said, "There is never any question whether a book is there, only making it available to yourself." Do you still believe that?*

WS: I think so. Some people have means of finding stories and some people don't. I get a hundred letters a year from people who read *Angle of Repose* and write to say, "I've got my grandmother's diary and she lived a very exciting life. I've always . . . but I can't do it. Wouldn't *you* like to do it?" It's not for me unless I find it in myself. *They* feel it as a book, but they can't write it. *I* might be able to write it, but I don't feel it as a book.

NB: *Do you have any idea how they might make that material available to themselves?*

WS: One of the things you have to do is simply submit to the time in front of the typewriter or desk every day. The number of hours spent writing a book is quite incredible. You write every page of every book seven or eight times—every page probably represents a day's work, at eight hours a day—and if you've got a four hundred or five hundred page book, that's thousands of hours. Most people don't have that much time or won't spend it writing. So you have to reassure yourself every morning that what you're doing isn't insane; only then would you go through all the trouble of making a book. If a book could be made in two hours, like a watercolor picture, lots of people would write books; but the plain duration of writing a novel discourages most people.

NB: In The Writer in America *you say that since almost every cultural force pushes your students in the direction of commercialization, "Let the colleges stand up for art."*

WS: Many of the people who went through our shop wound up in advertising, publishing, or movies, and all of those are commercial aspects of writing in which someone gives them an assignment and they turn it out. But it does seem useful to young writers, for a year or two, to be in a completely uncommercial atmosphere where they can write anything their minds suggest to them. That's the best way to develop as a writer. People learn much writing to order, but they learn more writing what they want. Most students in a writing program are not going to be important writers, but many of them look back on those years as a time when, for once in their lives, education was exactly what they wanted it to be: when they got none of the dictation from without that they might have resented, when only help came from without. So we give fellowships to ensure that some of these people can write exactly what they want for a year or two, and still eat. And over the now more than thirty years, the policy has justified itself.

Every year former students come to me for blurbs, and I generally have to beg off: I can't read that many books. I read for the National Book Award the last year it was given. We read over two hundred books and of those two hundred, twenty-two were by my former students. That's one-tenth of American Literature. There aren't any Saul Bellows among those people, but there are National Book Award Winners and Harper Prize Winners and Pulitzer Prize Winners: Scott Momaday, Bob Stone, Tom McGuane, Ernest Gaines,

Evan Connell, Ed Abbey, Larry McMurtry, Wendell Berry . . . There's a whole string of them through the years, and many of them go on producing steadily.

We didn't ever try to make publishing a condition. Nothing should be written for a specific audience—its vocabulary reduced to six hundred words for the sixth grade audience, or whatever else. Schoolteachers often make the mistake of trying to limit vocabulary to accommodate bad readers with the result that they limit it for everybody. If you read Dickens when you're seven years old, you're going to be stretched; he didn't limit his vocabulary. And stretching is useful. Aiming a manuscript at a particular audience is never justifiable except on commercial terms, and those are the least useful guidelines for writing well. I suppose if you're writing true confessions for some lurid magazine, you have to do them in a certain way; but real writing is not done by mass production out of interchangeable parts. That's the way they make automobiles, not the way they make stories or novels.

On the other hand, if you're a writer, you're a man or a woman in search of an audience, and when you publish something, that means you've found your audience. So in our classes, everyone was greatly cheered whenever anybody in the class sold a story to a magazine or a novel manuscript to a publisher. That's somehow what it was all about, even though it wasn't cued to those cues. It was written in what the writer felt was the right way. Then when somebody likes it, that's fine. The writer hasn't prostituted himself at all.

NB: You've suggested that the most fundamental instruction in literature takes place in writing classes.

WS: I'm not sure that literature classes—I may be speaking heresy here—fully justify themselves. Anybody with brains can read and understand a book, and if he doesn't understand it, he knows where to get the books that will help him understand it. I've seen students learn more about literature by hearing Frank O'Connor read a chapter out of *Portrait of the Artist as a Young Man* in his rich Irish brogue than by all the analysis and exegesis and lectures that scholars have devoted to that book. When it's read like that, it's alive, and a manuscript is still alive and still malleable when you're working on it, or when you're trying to help someone else make it the way he wants to make it. If you just read literature and never have the experience of trying to make it, it's a monument; but a writer knows that when it was being made, every word was debatable. Literature can be taught in different ways, but the routine grinding out either of literary history or of *explication de texte* is not as much fun or as rewarding as trying to make literature yourself in a congenial group, with a teacher who is neither too soft nor too hard, and with enough to eat.

NB: *In* The Big Rock Candy Mountain, *a professor's wife who has been reading Lewis suggests that academics are Babbitts.*

WS: I may have been blowing off steam, I suppose, when I wrote that.

NB: *Maybe you had been grading themes at Wisconsin because it sounds like that's what her husband does.*

WS: I may have been. I was grading them at Harvard, too. One had plenty of opportunity to teach Freshman English. In many ways, the best class I ever taught, too. It was a writing class of a kind; you were dealing with things in their malleable state. When the war came, the young instructors went off to the Army and Navy, and all the old gray-beard professors had to take over Freshman English. I remember Hyder Rollins, a linguist, coming in puzzled after his first two or three meetings of Freshman English saying, "What is the subject matter of this course?" You had to tell him, *(laughter)* "It's what you make it; it's what you can get out of them." Freshman English is a more challenging course than one on the glosses of Gabriel Harvey or something like that. It's much less definite. When you're a young instructor, you're always being bitter and witty at the expense of Freshman English. Later on, you may change your mind. I was pretty young when I wrote that book.

NB: *What's the difference between expository writing and fiction?*

WS: For one thing, expository writing has to contain a body of information. But that body of information doesn't have to be blunt or obtuse. It doesn't hurt any writer of expository prose to try his hand at writing a story, because control of place and character and evocation of sensuous impressions and so on, are all things that can be used in expository writing. You shouldn't write fiction when you're doing expository writing, but you may use many of the devices and shapes and implements and weapons of fiction.

NB: I looked at an expository writing text that a group of you put together.

WS: *Exposition Workshop.* It was a casebook on controversies designed for Freshman English classes where you had to give a bunch of reluctant people something to write about. Claude Simpson, Stuart Brown, and I were teaching Freshman English in the middle of the depression, and we thought that since everything was being questioned and torn apart and refinished and refurbished, we would make a textbook which took certain controversies, a controversial program like the WPA's Writers Project, say, and put together a collection of articles around them. We thought if we gave the students conflicting ideas, maybe we'd knock off some sparks. It was only a theory.

NB: I thought I found something you wrote: "To write something, it has been said, is to perform an act of knowing."

WS: I suppose I did write that. I wrote the term paper too. We took them through the process of making a term paper: "It begins with these little loose cards, and then it gradually proceeds to some sort of orderly statement."

NB: You were also involved in producing a writing book where people talked about how they wrote their stories.

WS: That was an attempt to get behind the story and make it seem less like a monolith, less like a fixed and immutable thing and more like something a mind had worked on and chiseled. We tried to find stories that their authors had talked about; when we couldn't, we ourselves talked about how they were made.

NB: Your own writing shows that no story is a monolith. I read Recapitulation *before I read* The Big Rock Candy Mountain, *but it took me a while to realize that they were about the same people.*

WS: I wrote *Recapitulation* in other terms, not as a trailer to *The Big Rock Candy Mountain* at all. Then, because it concerned the same period and a couple of short stories that had been spin-offs from *The Big Rock Candy Mountain* were buried in it, it kept wanting to be a trailer to *The Big Rock Candy Mountain.* So, eventually, I rewrote it and changed all the names and some of the stories to fit the new names. But I didn't do it that way at first. I wrote it in the first person singular with a different character in mind. And then because those two short stories kept flowing back toward the character which could have been Bruce Mason, I thought I might as well just call him that.

NB: You've written so much. Everyone who knew I was going to talk to you said, "I read the most wonderful book by Wallace Stegner," and it was always a different book.

WS: (*Laughter.*) You live a long time, that's how . . .

NB: And they were all different kinds of books.

WS: They ought to be different; you ought to change. But some of them are kind of alike. Two, for instance, are written about and around this hill: *All the Little Live Things* and *The Spectator Bird* use the same character, the same setting and some of the same ideas. *Big Rock Candy Mountain* and *Recapitulation* are alike in some sense; *Recapitulation* is a continuation of the same story and a retelling of part of the story from an altogether different point of view. But *Angle of Repose* is different in that it's partly historical. And there is one novel about New Hampshire which is quite different because it exploits a different area and lingo than any of my other novels.

NB: Editing DeVoto's letters and putting together Wolf Willow *are different again.*

WS: *Wolf Willow* has the same relation to *The Big Rock Candy Mountain* that *Life on the Mississippi* has to *Huckleberry Finn,* to put myself in good company. It was a nonfictional treatment of much of the same stuff that the novel used.

NB: Do you do different things at once?

WS: Oh, no.

NB: Or do you float from one to another or get interested in one and . . .

WS: Either way. I don't know how books grow, but they have a seedtime and a growing time and a harvest time, like other plants.

Sometimes you have to dig up a subject and sometimes you don't know where you're going when you start. You start it and it wants to go another way; you resist, and very often it goes its own way in spite of you. But it had better not go entirely its own way, because then you're out of control. For instance, I wrote *Wolf Willow* as a bunch of chapters, magazine articles, because I got the feeling that I ought to become the Herodotus of the Cypress Hills; nobody had ever written a history of that country. Now I find that I *am* the Herodotus; I'm required reading in Canada. *(Laughter.)* Finally, having gotten a whole mess of chapters together, I began to realize it was a book; but I still didn't know how to put it together. It ended ineptly and inconclusively and I couldn't tell what was wrong with it. I gave it to Malcolm Cowley and he said, "Why don't you just move this chapter from the front to the back?" That's all it took!

That story "Genesis," about the cowpunchers running a fall roundup and getting into a succession of blizzards, was written because I didn't want to write as pure exposition stuff that I felt and remembered so vividly. So I chose to write it as fiction, which screwed up the book and made it a librarian's nightmare.

NB: *Why?*

WS: How to catalogue it. *(Laughter.)* But I couldn't finish "Genesis." I got the cowpunchers to the place where their sled is broken down in the rapids and they make their way to a line camp, and I couldn't take it on. I put the thing away for at least a year and then I took it out and realized that I hadn't been able to finish it because it *was* finished. It didn't want to be a novel about the whole winter; it just wanted to be an episode about the making of a boy into a man. An ordeal story like that never wants to be as long as you think it might be; it has to be long enough to be a real ordeal, but not so long that it becomes excruciating. I wanted to make it excruciating and I couldn't do it.

NB: *It must be hard to let books happen like that if you write for a living.*

WS: When you write for a living you have to write a lot of things that didn't get generated in your own head. I've written travel articles on assignment, but I've never done it with fiction. I don't think I could. Writing for a living gets a little easier as you get older and have more things in print—unless your past writing disappears from sight. But making a good living from writing means writing best-sellers and following them with best-sellers, which is very hard to do. Or it means writing for the magazines—to a degree, putting yourself in the hands of editors who tell you what to do. Or it means writing information or think pieces, or, in my case, travel or environmental pieces which express something of what I think, but are more salea-ble to the magazines than other kinds of things. So I write many pieces about the public domain. I'm writing one now. I retired from teaching ten years ago. I've written for a living ever since. A com-plete living. It's a very speculative life.

NB: Are you getting more writing done since you've stopped teach-ing?

WS: I don't think so; I just write a little more steadily. I tried to spend the morning writing and do the university's business in the afternoon and evening, but that wasn't always possible. So I might get in two hours instead of four; but now that I'm not doing anything else, I can do my own business for four hours or more a day. Four is about enough. I do it seven days a week, and that eventually adds up to some pages.

NB: In The Writer in America, *you said that the fear universities would smother writers has been shown false.*

WS: It depends on the writer. The universities have smothered some writers; they've made academics out of some writers, and that isn't always the best thing for a writer, or a critic. The New Critics got tainted by the academy too; they were a little too remote and monastic and concerned so rigorously with the text that they forgot texts come out of contexts. Books come out of contexts too, and if the experience within the university is the only experience a writer has, it's going to be a little narrow. On the other hand, there's Jane Austen. *(Laughter.)* You can find plenty of people who have written well out of narrow experience, so it's not a uniform reaction. Some writers have been in teaching more or less all their lives: Saul Bellow, Red Warren, myself—there are all kinds of us. We haven't stopped writing and I don't know that we're any worse writers for having been in the academy; some of us may be better.

NB: Then why did you write an essay advising a young writer to avoid teaching?

WS: She has to have it all polished to a fingernail. That's nice, but it means enormous work on every sentence. You can't do that while you're looking at someone else's sentences. That's something I'm glad to be rid of. Frank O'Connor and I agreed that when we got more excited about someone else's story than our own, we were in trouble. He was always half-hinting that I ought to quit teaching, and he was probably right.

NB: Because you get too involved?

WS: You *do* get involved, particularly when they're good students and you like them. You're very concerned to see them succeed with what they're doing; but you do, then, lose your own singlemindedness.

NB: And writing travel articles does not interfere as much because they flow out of your own interests?

WS: Travel is not unrelated to fiction; it's the place of fiction without the fiction in it. Sometimes you add a little fiction, a little autobiographical travel account. When I get broke, I can always write a travel piece; a lot of travel pieces turn into ecological and environmental pieces because so many places one travels these days show the marks of human carelessness.

NB: In The Sound of Mountain Water *you say, "As a novelist, I may perhaps be forgiven for taking literature as a reflection, indirect but profoundly true, of our national consciousness; and our literature, perhaps you are aware, is sick, embittered, losing its mind, losing its faith."*

WS: That was written about 1960, when almost every novel you picked up was concerned with aberrations of experience instead of the real lives of real people. It was a literature of perpetual losers, and everybody who wasn't a loser turned out to be the villain who made the loser lose. I don't believe that. So I was disturbed that fiction portraying psychological alienation seemed to take precedence over that describing lives which had some stability in them, and which arrived somewhere, did something—not much, maybe, but something.

DIANE WAKOSKI

NB: In your essay on form and content you talk about the need for a writer to develop honest self-awareness and then somehow transmute that into form. Does that idea influence the way you teach?

DW: The only writers that really interest me are the ones who are original and I think their originality almost always comes out of an organically honest expression of [their] involvement with the world, so I am most interested in writers who are honest creators of their own myth. Even if you're not going to become [a] great writer, you'll become a better writer if you become a very, very honest perceiver of the world and I don't see any way for doing that unless you're a very mean and honest perceiver of yourself. I'm always urging searching the self and trying to come to terms with what you find there.

NB: Do you urge your students to do that?

DW: Oh yes, and I encourage the kind of writing that does that. I will not let my workshops be therapy sessions, no way. I will never let the writing be treated as therapy. I'm a brutal critic precisely because I don't want people to do it just for an ego trip. The writing should be an ego trip and coming to terms with it should be an intellectual one. I'm not gratuitously mean, but I am very honest about my responses. It's true I don't have everybody's responses, but I have good critical responses.

One of the ways I come to terms with this for students is by being very hard on them for writing clichéd or sentimental things because, as far as I'm concerned, things you don't have enough experience with are going to be in other people's terms, thus clichéd. I don't think it's enough just to honestly record your emotions. It's important to look for the most important and deep emotions you have. It's important to look for the conflicts. Good writing is always about problems and conflict. It isn't about easy or easily accessible things, so it means digging down. I'm very critical of being superficial; I'm even critical of so-called good writing if it doesn't seem to be yielding anything very exciting or interesting.

I have many kinds of students, but in terms of language, I really do have two kinds of students and I'm more successful dealing with the kind that has read a lot and has [a] rich vocabulary and a good sense of language, but still hasn't learned a personal way of using it —hasn't learned how to get rid of clichés, sentimental speech. The other students have a very, very poor sense of language and from one standpoint, it's insane they should think of being writers of any kind *(laughter)* because the more you purify [their] speech, the more you get down to a very debased speech with poor vocabulary and not a very accurate sense of the world. I have one device for dealing with those students psychologically—this sounds horrible, but it's true— which is to make them hate their language and make them want to read and learn another language.

NB: How do you do that?

DW: It usually involves making them hate themselves. It's a horrible burden to take upon yourself and I've only done it successfully with a few students and those are the ones that are determined to stick with me and to come back. Most students have no intellectual or emotional honesty that equips them to deal with that problem of hating yourself and then rallying that hate to change, so I mainly work with students who already have a sense of language and need a tutor or model to constantly be pointing out where their sense of language is deserting them.

In advanced workshops I almost always require at least one piece of writing and encourage two. I have the luxury of very small classes and we meet once a week for a long session, three to four hours, which means I can talk about everybody's poems or poem in detail using that *explication de texte* method. I point out where they are working well with language, but frequently they're not working well with language and I spend a lot of time talking about clichés and sentimentality, sentimental ideas as much as sentimental use of language, but I keep trying to emphasize that if you learn to use language with purity, verve and power, you can handle even a sentimental idea. I encourage them to get away from sentimental, clichéd thinking and I talk a lot about thinking.

NB: How?

DW: My first comment on a poem may be about the idea behind the poem. We may talk for fifteen minutes about the various ways people have used that idea, of how impossible it is to use in the twentieth century, where it comes in terms of other literature.

NB: Do you require them to read?

DW: It's not fair to ask students in a writing class to do a lot of reading, but my theme song from beginning to end, every day, is that you will never be a good writer unless you read a lot. I have what I call my literacy list of twentieth-century poets that everyone should know; I read contemporary poetry and talk about it a little in my classes. In no way do I feel that I'm trying to give a remedial reading course because I know there's not time, but I keep pointing out that if you read more poetry, you couldn't write like this.

I have taken to assigning one oral book review that I give them no models for and don't grade them on. It requires that you read one whole work by a contemporary poet on my list. If you want to do serious writing about poetry today, you're better off writing book reviews than critical articles because there are plenty of places to publish them and they can do more good because they might help somebody sell a book. My rule of thumb is that you should try to be as literate as if you were writing a critical article, but you don't have to have spent your life studying that poet; you're permitted to make judgements that come out of the fact that you've only read one book. Sometimes it makes me squirm when I realize they don't have any idea what a book review sounds like. I toy with bringing in book reviews and giving them oral book reviews, but I feel it should be up to them to make some of those conclusions. I am constantly struggling with the battle between that parental feeling of wanting to show somebody how to do it right and feeling that if they don't learn how to do it on their own, then all I'm doing is giving them one model for behavior that helps prevent them from using their minds.

NB: In Toward a New Poetry, *you say "a lot of just plain bad language and adolescent or old-fashioned ideas have to be written through to get to the place where the slow process of revision will make a poem better rather than just different." How does that idea influence your teaching?*

DW: I do think writing your way through a lot of junk is very important, and I don't have any good advice about how to handle that in the classroom; I don't know how you get around the problem in class of having. . . . Well, let me give you an example of a problem I've had this year. This is in my so-called advanced undergraduate poetry writing workshop and so this student has previously taken at least one other poetry writing workshop. It's hard to tell that from anything he writes; he writes very, very poorly. His ideas are so clichéd, that he makes a television news commentator sound like he has brilliant, original ideas. His use of cliché is worse than the way most of us speak every day. Why this boy wants to write poetry, I don't know; but I don't feel it's my business to discourage him from it. It is my business to try to get him to write something more interesting. His one saving grace is that he really wants to write poetry and he wrote more than the required poems, not twice as many, which a good student often does, but more than the ten required for the ten week term. That's a sign of an ambitious, serious student. Now it's true that he's lazy, that he writes them in five minutes; but many of the other students write theirs in five minutes too, but they only turn in one every two weeks, and so this boy does have something on his side.

This boy came to two classes and got lambasted for five poems that had no saving grace in them. He was absent from another class—I later found out because he was "so discouraged"—and then came to the next class and had about three more poems. One of them had a tiny glimmer of hope in it. He used specifics. They weren't very good, but at least he was not generalizing his way out into total oblivion. So I praised him highly for at last doing something worthwhile in a poem and then went on to say that the beginning was terrible and the ending was terrible and the whole idea, if he really meant what he said, was ridiculous; but those specifics were really nice.

He asked if he could see me in my office, which he did the next day, and he said, "It was so wonderful. At last you praised me. At last I begin to feel that there's hope and that maybe now I can send something out and get published." So I listened to him for a while, basically, the psychiatrist listening to this sad sack personality, and I said, "Well, you wouldn't want me to praise you if it were a lie, would you?" And I could see that he wanted to say, "Yes" *(laughter),* but he didn't dare because he knew that would provoke great anger from me and this is a person who's used to getting along in the world. So I said, "Look, you're out of touch with reality. Your poetry is no more ready for publication than I'm ready to go to the Olympics in high diving; I can't swim. I tried to praise something you were doing because you were on the right track. Your problem is that you're lazy; you want instant gratification for very little work." I talked to him for a long, long time about this and it made him feel better to have someone talking to him. I kept trying to emphasize what he could do and how he could work and how he needed to take an idea and develop it and that he was kidding himself if he felt that all his best ideas came when he was walking along the street and didn't have a pencil. I said, "If that's the case, carry a pencil and a notebook, but I think you'll find you'll jot something down and won't have any idea what it means, that your problem is you don't take the ideas you have and develop them using these very simple specifics."

The next class session, for some reason *(laughter)* that I will never know, he had a poem that was praiseworthy. And I praised it. It wasn't a great poem, but it was a nice beginner's poem. I pointed out what he did that succeeded and also, somewhat painfully, [contrasted] that with what he had done so much that didn't succeed. He glowed all through class and I thought, that's nice; maybe that pep talk helped.

The next week he came to class and he had no poem because he said he didn't dare risk having something fail after his success. And he never wrote anything for the rest of the term. *(Laughter.)* It made me have great faith in my technique of telling people how terrible they are because, while they rant and rave, I feel more and more and more and more and more that we sell our *souls* for these educational ideas of encouraging students out of fear that they'll go away and never come back. My experience has been that the good students go away and never come back because they've proven to themselves they can get praise. I see many of the most talented students I've had in class a few years later. What are they doing? "Oh, I'd like to make a movie." "Oh, I'm working for an advertising agency." "Do you write poetry?" "Oh, no." Maybe the thing that keeps people going as students is the desire to accomplish something. Maybe that easy success is as much a cut-off of a person's life of learning—especially if it's false or it means something very small—as someone like me who's always being accused of discouraging people.

I think this student is very, very typical of the creative writing student you get in high school, that you get in all beginning courses. He was really laying it on the line to me what the average student wants from a writing teacher: "Please praise me. Please praise me." And their excuse is, "I'm doing this for pleasure. Why should you make it painful?"

I gave a one afternoon workshop this spring, and one young woman said she had taken a poetry workshop in college and the teacher had been so harsh it had totally discouraged her and she hadn't come back to poetry for years. I said, "Well, are you writing now?" And she said, "Yes." And I said, "Maybe you needed that time to come back to a place where you were ready to write." Well, she wasn't having any of this. She said, "Oh no, it just discouraged me so much; it took me this long to get my courage back up." I said, "I don't know anything about you or your writing, but I'd like to give a big hooray for your teacher because your teacher probably stopped you from something that, if she had praised you, you'd still be doing today and it probably was very bad writing. Sometimes you have to go away from something in order to learn to come back to it with intelligence and skill. I don't think that everything you do in life is one continuous process. You may have been way off on the wrong track or you may have been stupid or you may have been ungifted; you may still be." She stared at me. And I said, "I know you think that teacher did something very terrible to you, but she may have given you a gift. She may have turned you into a real writer." There was silence after this and I decided I'd better change the subject and I did. But there is too much of this sense we have to make everybody love everything.

A young woman I had in a writing class kept saying to me, "How can you give me a 1.0 and mark up the whole page: 'clichéd,' 'sentimental,' 'bad writing,' 'awkward.' I have always been told that I'm very talented as a poet. I won poetry prizes in high school and my teacher thought I was the best student she'd ever had." This girl was too diplomatic to say, "You're a bad teacher" *(laughter),* but her complaint was all saying, "What right do you have to say these things?" This was the third week of her complaints about this; I was sick of them and she's intelligent so she could learn to write better —but you don't learn to write better until you become dissatisfied with what you're doing. I said, "Look, don't you know by now that ninety percent of the world *hates* poetry? They not only don't read it, they dislike it when they read it and they will tell you anything to get rid of you. As soon as you understand that the only standards in poetry are those held by the few of us who really love it and probably write it, then you'll be ready to write good poetry." She looked as if I'd vomited all over her, which I had, in an intellectual sense. I don't know if she believed me or not, but I hope this girl won't write any poetry for ten years. I hope she'll come back to it as an intelligent reader who through something in her life has really come back to poetry and not this ghastly, nauseous, adolescent, roses are red, swooning violets, worse than Hallmark Cards stuff.

NB: So you don't think the primary issue is getting your students in touch with themselves?

DW: I think the primary issue is getting one's deepest self in touch with that most outside the self, what poetry is. I don't think that by searching through the history of poetry you're going to come to good poetry any more than I think that just by searching down into your self . . .One of the reasons I talk about honesty is I think you have to strip away everything except your real attitudes both towards what you read and your feelings about yourself and life before you can start making some harmonious connection between the two. I *would* rather work with a student who has read a million poems and isn't in touch with himself because it seems much easier in this society to help a person get in touch with himself *(laughter)* than to get in touch with literature. On the other hand, I think they have to be an equal process. I'm no more hopeful for the person who just wants to grub around in his interior and has no sense of art and language than I am for the person who's way out there in some lofty, ethereal, linguistic realm that has nothing to do with humanity. It's a problem of trying to get the interior and exterior in touch with each other and this is where a lot of teachers fall into the trap of wanting to be therapists because, in a sense, it's the same job: helping to integrate personalities.

NB: I was interested by your remark that writers shouldn't need therapy because that's what they do all the time.

DW: I don't believe writing is therapy; I think writing is therapeutic in the sense that good writing is an act of balancing, harmonizing, understanding, putting things together, creating a whole, understanding the incomplete in order to be complete. We don't live our art, so probably your art is more whole than you are. You're in total control of your art and you're not totally in control of your life. There are all those other people in your life—from the income tax person, to your wife or children—who have heavy holds on your life, and you have almost total control over your poems which is such a wonderful reality. But I would think just being in touch with the wholeness would give you a kind of wholeness in your life.

NB: Then why the myths about writers being temperamental and selfish?

DW: Anyone who is an artist has trained himself and also simply allows himself to keep his senses and his emotions on top of everything else because that's how he records what he's going to use— whether he's a painter, musician, poet—and I think that on one level makes him very vulnerable, and on another level, gives him a privilege that many people envy because he's allowed to be a child in the sense that he's allowed to live for his emotions and his feelings. Well, when you look at it, he isn't really allowed to any more than a banker is allowed to live with money. He's made that his definition of his life and he's going to fight for it. That's where he becomes selfish.

NB: That need to make one's feelings primary is supposed to have given a lot of women writers trouble.

DW: Why?

NB: Because we live in a culture that doesn't take women seriously, and that doesn't encourage women to take themselves seriously, espe-

cially as writers. Well, you know there aren't a whole lot of women poets who've done as well as you have.

DW: One of the reasons I dislike being associated with the feminist movement, besides the fact that I'm not political, is that I don't identify with most of the problems women in the women's movement have. I don't discredit them or discount them or *any* of those things; those just haven't been my problems. My undergraduate years at Berkeley, I didn't have any trouble being accepted as the leader of the pack in the poetry world. I enjoyed being in a world where there were more men than women because I didn't find it easy to meet people and so it created a world of men for me. I don't feel like they treated me differently because I was a woman or any of those things; I very early felt that the writing world was a heterosexual world. Josephine Miles was one of the poetry teachers who was a successful poet at Berkeley when I was there. She certainly didn't have any problems other than her lifetime arthritis, so if anything she was treated like a cripple, but she was one of those brave cripples who could do more things and did more things than most people who had normal bodies. *(Laughter.)* Maybe I've always been around people who assumed that they had to prove themselves in the world and that was normal.

Whatever my psychological problems were, they came more from coming from a lower-class family, or uneducated people; they came from growing up without a father, from poverty, etc. I was always considered lucky because I was smart and was good at school and I took great pride in having those brains. The world of poetry was a world that relieved me from the world of poverty, that could create friendships for me; it created an involvement not only with people that interested me, but an intellectual life and a sexual life and a romantic life. I not only didn't feel inferior, I felt superior because I was always good in school. The world of books and writing was my world.

The women's problems I've had been been sexual. How do you have a sex life without birth control, which is what girls were stuck with in the fifties. What if you don't believe in marriage? When I was young, I don't think I believed in marriage; I now do, but certainly not in a conventional way. All the men I lived with during the fifties and part of the sixties and had to pretend I was living alone because if I told people at my job, I didn't know what would happen because it just wasn't . . . and all those lies you have to tell and all the miseries of that life. Those are the horriblenesses of the failure of the sexual revolution; they don't have anything to do with being yourself or certainly don't have anything to do with careers or making money. If I've gotten involved with men who were my intellectual inferiors or who don't have jobs or who have emotional problems, that came from my experience of growing up without a father and not knowing how to relate to men as my sexual, social equals; it has never had anything to do with my poetry life, my career life.

NB: My mother loves to say things like, "I wish I had the leisure to worry about doing something meaningful." Maybe she's onto something.

DW: Yes. It's a nice, healthy statement. *(Laughter.)*

NB: Maybe women have trouble writing because they think they don't have to make it as a poet or a novelist or whatever.

DW: Yes. I definitely think one of my advantages was growing up poor because I didn't have a lot of those bourgeois assumptions, not only about marriage, but about careers. There was nobody else's success hanging over my head if I failed. I think my contemporaries who have very successful parents or even middle-class parents and the kids I see in college now with their successful, affluent parents, have the knowledge that there's no clear road for them to go out in the world and do as well as their parents did. Maybe they're the first generation that can't even dream of going beyond their parents, so it's much harder and creates a different kind of striving. And, of course, the heart of the women's movement is these upper-middle-class wives who, by my standards, have lived easy, pleasant, good lives and have been given the pip that they're so dissatisfied. Go out and do something if you want to do it. You have all that free time, you have money, you have emotional support. Why do you want to rebel?

I've recently been reading all of Gail Godwin's novels and she writes about that middle-class world, but she writes with the panache of a Southern writer, so the character is so bizarre that you don't get irritated that she's having middle-class housewife blues. They're fascinating books. They make me realize how different I am from all those people. I would never have taken on a married lover. The idea of having an affair with someone who is married to someone else is really offensive to me and this is a person who has lived a sexual life that most people would not consider exactly proper and certainly not moral, but there's where my standards are. I meet middle-aged, attractive, well-kept, well-groomed women who are grousing about their handsome, nice husbands and having affairs and I feel no sense of sympathy or identification whatsoever. I feel like they've been given everything and now they want more. *(Laughter.)* The one thing society never takes away from you is the opportunity to create some kind of meaning for your life; I think a person who can't create meaning for his own life is a pretty poor excuse for a human being.

NB: When you say, "Poetry is as interesting as the poet," I'm not certain what you mean by "interesting." In one place you say that poets may have trouble writing when they get middle-aged because their lives are less interesting, but in another place you say a poet can make anything interesting.

DW: When you're young, sex is much more important in your life, money is more important in your life in the sense of worldly things, adventure, the people you meet, all those exterior things create your self in the world in your sense. Poetry comes very much out of those things: sexual encounters, a sense of everything about yourself that's exterior. When you get older, those things settle down a little bit and you turn inward.

It has strictly to do with having a young body as opposed to having an old body. And you move much more in an exterior way in that young body; as you get old, your body fails and so you move inside. It's not that you've never been in your head before, but there seems to be a direct pipeline between your head and your body when you're young.

NB: And your mind and your body become cut off from each other?

DW: Absolutely. I don't believe that this hulk I walk around in has anything to do with me.

NB: I do know that when I was younger a lot of external things that I knew weren't important mattered to me, like grades, what people thought . . .

DW: Right. And to the degree that you're a thoughtful person, you know when you're young that those grades didn't make a difference, you know if you're attracted to someone sexually, that doesn't necessarily mean anything, but that doesn't in any way counter the overwhelming physicality, external reality of how awful it would feel if you failed a course. You simply are a more exterior person when you're young.

When we're young, most of us write out of a much more exterior sense of the world and as we get older, our world gets more and more interior. If we're used to that exterior source, it's going to take a while to create the changeover into the interior. There may be a period of confused writing, a change of styles . . .   If you have made poetry out of an emotional life and your emotional life seems dull, then you have to start making it out of some other part of your life that seems more interesting.

Perhaps there are people who don't lose that exterior quality; probably those are people we say never grew up. And maybe there are people who have less of a sense of it and those are people who never live their lives. I don't think I'm talking about anything rare, exotic, peculiar to me. I will stick to my statement that poetry is as interesting as the poet who writes it.

There are lots of ways to be interesting. Some poems have a lot of exciting imagination and that's what grasps you in the poem; other poets have a sense of language that's unique and even when the ideas happen to be stupid, the language grips you; other people have a sensuous sense of the world that's compelling and interesting and the ideas and the language are dull. But if there's nothing there . . . When I look at students' poems, I say, "Look, there are a hundred ways of making a good poem, but if a poem doesn't have any interesting ideas, doesn't have any interesting language, isn't sensuous, doesn't have any interesting images and doesn't have an interesting story, what does it have?" *(Laughter.)* It has to be interesting in some way. I can't say to this boy who wants to write poetry who doesn't have anything to say, "You aren't interesting enough to write poetry," because maybe he'll find a way. But I feel those people who find a way don't become great poets because the poetry is as interesting as the person who writes it and if you didn't have an interesting life in the first place, [you're] going to be [one of] the John Hall Wheelocks.

NB: One person I interviewed said it's important for writers to have some kind of cultural shift in their lives, that someone who went from prep school to Yale to Harvard Law School would write less interestingly about Yale than someone who went from Yale to Vista.

DW: It's not only where material comes from, it may also be where the motivation to write comes from. If your life has been in a straight line, then you can only consider writing part of that straight line. It's not that you don't have anything interesting to write about, but you may not have the motivation to write about it. When people's lives take interesting turns, something happens where the straight line stops; that's often when they get the urge to write.

NB: You've said that the beginning of poetry is having something to say.

DW: Sure.

NB: A lot of the people I talked with said the opposite, that a young poet should love language more than ideas. And some think literature teachers concentrate too much on content.

DW: There's no doubt that the problem of poetry is the problem of language, but the poem is an extension of content—I stick with that old Creeley maxim. It seems more and more true every year and a more and more true way of studying the great contemporary poetry. I don't see how you can talk about form until you see it wedded with content. I don't see how you can have a poet who loves language, who has nothing to say, whereas, I do see how you could have a poet who has something to say even if his language is limited. The nature of language changes so quickly, almost by definition, each of us is dated. What we're all searching for is immortality and immortality of language has to be deeply wedded with content or the language has no meaning.

If language is always changing, we live in a time when it's even more rapidly changing because of television and fashions in language change even faster. If there's a hip way to talk this year, it's different by next year. I suspect in the beginning of the twentieth century, language fashions at least lasted for four or five years. Now we're lucky if they last four or five months. You'd think that rapidity of change would make people more sensitive to language, but, in fact, what it does is desensitize people to language, so in one sense, it hardly matters what the other one says. I think the poets you heard saying, "It's the language," are responding to that problem in students. And so they may be misrepresenting what they really think of poetry if you isolate that out. They might not emphasize that nearly so much if they were living in a nonteaching context. Remember, most teachers of writing see people at the beginning of their writing, when they're least sensitive to language; by the time you become sensitive to language, you can be your own teacher and go out in the world. All of us who put ourselves in the position of teachers, including those who are teaching on the graduate level in American universities, are seeing people at the beginning of their skills and that has to be an assault on a poet's ear. So I suspect when we start articulating some of those things, we're creating a kind of balance for ourselves that has to do with that life.

NB: What did you mean when you said, "It is a craft that you can only teach by example"?

DW: One of the reasons people are so interested in artists' lives is a sense that there is something almost impossible to articulate that's been directly conveyed from the artist into the art and that you don't always see it, or, if you see it, you don't understand it or why it's there. That's one of the reasons we like to have poets reading their own poems and one of the reasons people like to see painters or musicians on talk shows; in the world of popular music this is extended into the musician singing his own song. There is a sense that there is something magical that the artist has that he is transforming into art, but sometimes it's locked into the art object. Not everybody walks through a museum and sees anything magical in the paintings. Some people find them dead and boring. Some people want to find something there and don't, so they take art appreciation courses. Not everybody goes to a concert and hears a great violinist and perceives it as great or hears a piece of music and is overwhelmed by the magic in it. What's even more disconcerting is that the very piece of literature you found magical at one point isn't magical the next time you read it. This means that the art object does have some mysterious connection with something, either the artist or history or something.

If it were just a matter of perfect form, we could teach that. But we don't even agree what perfect form is and we can't even agree that the concept of perfect form is a beautiful concept. There's a wonderful David Ignatow poem dedicated to a nameless poet who received a major prize with the designation that the poet was receiving the prize for creating poems of perfect form. It's a short satirical poem where he says, over and over again, all the things that don't have perfect form:

> Hello, dead, napalmed man, can you become a
>   poem of perfect form?
> Hello, incinerated Jew, can you become a
>   poem of perfect form? . . .
> If you can't make yourself a poem of perfect form
> then you have no right to be in this country.

It makes you aware that not even artists will agree among themselves what makes a great work of art and the more you pin people down, the more you see how individual response to a work of art becomes and how unnecessary to have a group or social world that teaches you, "Well, you may not like Picasso, but this is what Picasso is doing that's valuable and you can learn to see this abstractly."

NB: I heard you read some poems at the Modern Literature Conference and for some reason, I got angry. I wasn't angry at you, but those poems must have stirred something. I spent the next two weeks trying to figure out what made me mad.

DW: Did you figure it out?

NB: No, and I put off reading your poems. When I did read them, I liked them. I even saw an image from one of my dreams in one, but I do need to read them again more slowly and more carefully. I was misled by the poems you read because they made me think your poetry would be simpler than it is.

DW: I think it's the beguilement of the poetry reading. One of the reasons I think poetry readings are wonderful but deceptive is that all poetry seems immediately permeable when you hear the poet reading it. I'm particularly interested in the plain surfaces because of my didactic interest in being American; I think the true American language as opposed to the English language is a very smooth-textured, simple-seeming surface. My poetry is super beguiling because I do write in a very plain, rhetorical style that's suited for reading aloud.

I have that same feeling of anger at poetry readings and I finally analyzed that for the most part [it] is jealousy, not just because I'm a poet, but the feeling that person is getting total attention for the interior which is something we all want. I think that's a very true response and I distrust anyone who doesn't have it. For years I've been trying to understand why poetry is and always has been as unpopular as it is. There are lots of reasons. One is that it is written by an intellectual elite and so it presents a very complex reality and few people are meant to read it. But there's something else about this response of yours that may be even truer, because people don't say they don't like philosophy, they just don't read it. Whereas, they're always very apologetic: "I really don't like poetry." I think a lot of people have this feeling of jealousy, of "that person is saying what I should be saying; he has no right to be saying that." It may be the poet manqué in everyone saying, "Those are my feelings and ideas. What right does Rilke have to get attention for them?"

NB: Absolutely. There's nothing spookier than seeing your dream in someone else's poem.

DW: *(Laughter.)* Right, and they're getting lavish attention for it; you're getting nothing for it. *(Laughter.)*

NB: Maybe that's it, but I think I would find it very hard to publish, let alone read out loud, poems as personal as yours.

DW: There's another side. There's the jealousy where you wish you had something someone else has and I think that when that happens that's a true identification with the poem. There's the other side of that true identification that was revealed to me in a fan letter I got after *The Motorcycle Betrayal Poems* came out and really did get a lot of publicity. I got a letter from a man living somewhere around New York City saying, "Dear Diane Wakoski, I'm writing you this fan letter because I want to congratulate you on the success your new book is having, but at the same time, I wanted to tell you that some part of me wishes it were not. I have always felt like I knew you personally and that I was one of the few people who did. It's as if my lover is suddenly on the screen being made love to by someone else." I don't know if that was his image, but that's what he was talking about. He said, "I'm glad for you that people are reading your poems, but I don't like sharing you with all those people." I thought, that's a very, very true response. Literature is to us like making love and while some part of us wants the world to understand our beloved, some part of us wants to keep it locked away in a closet and be the only one who sees how beautiful it is. This is an explanation of why English teachers are seemingly perverse, dull people; they don't want to share that poetry with everybody. I understand that feeling very much. That's a true reader's feeling. The missionary feeling is the first feeling of joy when you want to tell everyone; then when you realize you're telling everyone, you want to take your words back. I think serious literature provokes a lot of personal feelings in us connected with our sense of identity, and all those crazy emotions that go with self: jealousy, privacy . . .

ANNE WALDMAN

NB: Would you please describe the St. Mark's Poetry Project?

AW: In the early sixties, poets had been having spontaneous gatherings (as I'm sure they've had for centuries), in Greenwich Village and there was a coffee house called The Metro on Second Avenue in the Lower East Side which housed weekly poetry readings. There was a falling out with the owners of that cafe, so the poets moved to the St. Mark's Church which had always traditionally been open to artists—Isadora Duncan had danced there, Harry Houdini once gave a magic demonstration and Frank Lloyd Wright lectured in it, just to mention a few notables. Then in 1966, a sociologist interested in working with alienated youth on the Lower East Side was able to raise a grant from the Office of Economic Opportunity to develop an arts program in that area, to be located at St. Mark's Church. He was able to raise enough money so that we could afford to pay twenty-five dollars a reading and have poets run workshops. There was also funding for a film project, the early Millennium Film Project, and a theater program, Theatre Genesis; so it was a lively and intensely productive scene.

Hundreds and hundreds of poets and writers have been through the St. Mark's Poetry Project reading their own work, teaching and participating in workshops and publishing in the Newsletter and *The World* magazine. Since the beginning, the Project had two weekly readings, four or five workshops running, a mimeo magazine, group readings, guest poets from other countries lecturing and reading. Marathon benefits at New Year's often go on all night or for two day stretches and involve many kinds of performers and artists as well:

145

dancers, musicians, filmmakers, singers. Yoko Ono and Patti Smith have both participated on occasion, for example. This is always quite an event with at least a thousand people in attendance. There is quite a colorful history to the Project as you can imagine.

The Project is very catholic in its range. When we first began, the idea was that the Church could provide a real and necessary arena for younger writers living in the lower east side community. It was truly a community operation: we had Ted Berrigan setting up the chairs on reading nights for $5.00. The staff consisted entirely of poets. That's why we had so much trouble: the dreamy poets were in charge! *(Laughter.)* You'd forget to put an ad in the newspaper and whose fault was it? Or the tape recorder wasn't turned on. But the original basis was the writing community's interest in inviting practically everyone out there known and unknown doing interesting work to come to this community spot. The audience was extremely important.

I was lured out to Naropa Institute in Boulder because it was so much like what I had been doing at St. Mark's and it seemed time to spread the energy and community a bit. I was first invited to Naropa in 1974 with Diane di Prima and Allen Ginsberg to do workshops and a reading. Naropa is a Buddhist inspired college, then just forming, and they knew that all three of us were interested and sympathetic and involved with Buddhist practice. Then we were further invited to create a poetics department. Diane and Allen and I stayed up hours, making copious lists for our fantasy poetry school —lists of all the people we wanted to invite and the kinds of teaching we wanted to evoke. We wanted active poets running and participating in the program. We asked John Cage about the workings of Black Mountain College and he said all the important exchanges and teachings had been accomplished at mealtimes!

NB: You've said that it was good for you to be taught by professional writers at Bennington. Why is that important?

AW: Professional, meaning "active," writers take what they're doing seriously and hopefully take their students seriously, take their students to heart. It would be boring for them if they were simply turning out dilettantes. I'm sure it was the same there as it is here: obviously, not everyone who comes here turns into a poet. If you

have one person out of ten who is still writing in twenty years . . .
I don't think you can really know after two or three years, or ten
years even, it's more like twenty, how far someone will go, how
they'll stick with it. But the idea was to scatter many seeds and
perhaps some would take root.

At Bennington Bernard Malamud was most attentive, concerned
and helpful, giving advice from his experience and from his heart.
Sometimes you could see right away that Howard Nemerov had been
in some intense creative state, had just written a poem. There was
a reading program at Bennington with many so-called academic
poets visiting. John Berryman, although inebriated much of his visit,
gave a brilliant, raggedy lecture on Pound and ended up passionately
reading Elizabeth Bishop's poem about the man who "lies in the
house of Bedlam," her poem about Ezra Pound at St. Elizabeth's
Hospital. Students often escorted the guest-poets about. Seeing Berryman, for example, in a very fragile state was touching and inspir-
ing. When I went out to the Berkeley poetry conference in 1965, it
was much the same: mixing with poets and seeing their fragilities,
seeing them in the process of living their work; there was no separation there. It was a sense of not compromising. Of doing something
outrageous for the love of the words and the music. I'm probably
being too romantic; I was seeing it all with younger eyes. Charles
Olson's presence there, his famous unveiling of himself, now historic,
was exceedingly powerful and moving.

NB: What's the value of seeing that fragility?

AW: You see that poets aren't fakes, aren't entertainers or politicians. They aren't handing you some obvious cynical "line." They
aren't manipulating language for devious ends. Their relationship to
language is a love affair. They've made a tremendous commitment
to the life and spirit of the language—the beauty of the language.
And there's a marvelous range of temperament amongst the poets.
I first heard Robert Lowell in 1961 or so, and his stance, his "music"
is so different from John Berryman's or Allen Ginsberg's. The range
is incredible which is why I don't like the labeling "schools." That's
so arbitrary and fuzzy. There is no method or system for how you
get to be a poet; it is very individual. You learn to rely on your own
mind, your own instincts, your own intuition and your own relation-

ship to the language. Somehow seeing that passion, that inspiration in other people was important to me. When I first heard Allen Ginsberg's vocalization of his own work, I was very excited. His encouragement when I was starting to read my work out loud was so helpful, his telling me to push to the limits and let go, trust my own sound and rhythm. Kenneth Koch also gave me encouragement.

NB: In an early interview, someone said that the most important thing he got from his teachers was validation.

AW: Right. I remember reading a poem called "100 Memories" which is a list poem and Kenneth (Koch) coming up afterward and saying, "Keep going with it; extend it" and "I love your vibrato." When I used to read in the early days, I was trembling and breathless; people would say, "It was very exciting, but are you all right? Maybe you should sit down, have a drink, take a cold shower?" Allen was so positive. I think a lot of the more excessive joyous poems came out of that affirmation that I was a poet. I was very nervous.

NB: And the same person said that when he teaches, he tries to validate his students in the same way, to say, "Not yet."

AW: Right. Or, "It's OK, but keep going further."

NB: Because that's more valuable than specific technical advice.

AW: Right. That's true. Many do not have the commitment but instead will be appreciators of poetry no matter what they do. It's one thing if they come to you with technical questions. Often I just want to affirm their commitment and demonstrate my own. Here at Naropa on the poetics faculty all of us work very differently as teachers. Allen Ginsberg and I agree on what should be taught, but we also diverge at certain points in terms of what we like in a poem and some students will work better with me and others better with him. It becomes an apprenticeship situation which is very, very particular. But that's part of the idea of our program: one-to-one "transmission." It's really so individual. What works or applies to one student may not apply to another.

We all might use William Carlos Williams to cut through the unfortunate haziness about what a poem is, and as a way of working with what you see in front of your nose, getting grounded in what's right here, right now and forgetting how your mother mistreated you decades ago or whatever. All of that can come back later if it really must be told, and probably in a more interesting way. Larry Fagin has all his students write a short autobiography first thing, to get that need to tell one's personal history out of the way. Once you've gotten that out of your system, you can start fresh.

We set up a situation which can allow the poems to materialize in various ways but also allow the students to stretch their muscles, try things out. Try writing a ballade, a sestina, a term paper!

We were also talking about a reading in which we'll work collaboratively with the music department, having students present their writing in collaboration with musicians. Allen loves doing that himself. One summer we had a forty-piece orchestra and he was up there conducting with a twig and singing and loving every minute of it.

NB: What do you try to do?

AW: Pass on the pleasure I get out of poetry. My husband (who also writes poetry) and I don't own a television, and since we've a baby, we don't go out excessively; so we frequently read aloud to each other—Homer, Shakespeare, James Schuyler, Laura Riding, Helen Adam. Attention to poetry of all kinds, ancient and modern, is very much part of our lives. I try to present the work that has inspired me hoping it will do the same for someone else: lift off the top of their heads a little.

I have an idea that there is some kind of muse or energy field, that some people can tap into. You can allow and create a space or atmosphere for those things to happen. "Words are forces the breath lets go," says Robert Duncan. So you organize your life and have poetry be a practice, a study, a discipline, as necessary as food, light, etc. and you give it back to the world.

Poets now are working in myriad ways. I've been making experimental poems where I weave together images and phrases from dreams or from journal notations. Those are like collages. Poems that come spontaneously are arriving in a different way, more mysteriously. Sometimes I'll want a poem that has a lot of diction in it or I'll flash on the shape of a poem first or a title or I'll read a poem by Yeats and get inspired by his stanza form. I decided in advance, for example, on a long form—twenty pages of five line verses: five verses a page. The poem came surprisingly fluently. Poems come in surprising ways and shapes and you prepare yourself for the hosting, so that you are ready to take in the poem. Is the poem interested in *us,* you wonder.

I'm very interested in getting people working spontaneously. I'm glad to look at their work, but I want to start from a fresh place. You might have an idea that poems have to include the blue sky and the clouds and the waves and the gulls and how great you feel that day: a lot of gush, usually. One sees that sentimentality a lot in early work. I've been teaching Gertrude Stein a good deal; you have to mention painting and music and bring up all kinds of things that get poetry out of its narrow compartment in talking about her work. I found that a woman in her sixties and a girl twelve years old were the most receptive to Stein's work. I think the woman in her sixties was completely open and wasn't hanging on to any preconceptions (her age made her wiser) and the twelve year old had an almost innate unconditioned understanding of Stein she maybe wouldn't have five years later. There are a lot of silly ideas about how you write a poem and not enough looking at your original mind. There's a way of cutting through that by experiments where you are brought into the moment confronted by your crazier or more interesting mind, and you are also more alert to what's around you—the world's more vivid.

Working with dreams can bring some of that out, although having everybody tell their dreams can be boring. Diane di Prima and I both use an exercise based on a Navajo ritual. You have one person sitting in the center of a room tell a dream and people walking around the person and absorbing the dream as it's being told, and moving, if they want, in a particular way inspired by the telling of it. Then you have them pick up on certain images, write them down, and use them in a piece of writing that can be "about" something else entirely. So the dreamer is sharing the dream and it's regurgitated by other people. It's an interesting way of starting a group working together, but it's also starting on the spot; one isn't bringing in preconceptions from years back, and you are using a common ground.

Another thing I've done is ask students to bring in objects that are relevant to them and have some history that they can relate. Everyone else takes notes and can ask questions about the objects and many stories come up that transcend the personal because the object keeps it away from "This is how I *feel* about that." Ego-centered work is a problem because everyone feels, "I'm a poet too and I have *my* story to tell." I get manuscripts from people who seem to be locked in their own preconceptions of what poems should be.

NB: *You mean they latch onto their . . .*

AW: Their private vision or neurosis or whatever . . .

NB: *So there has to be a balance between connecting to yourself and having a sense that someone else is out there?*

AW: Yes. Or being able to put the work outside yourself and look at it objectively. We often put the actual object on the table and so it removes the person in a way. It's almost a psychological exercise, but a lot of the writing is quite interesting. A student will come up with a detective story where these objects are clues toward some elaborate denouement. So then people are getting something out about themselves without going into a lot of psychoanalysis.

William Burroughs has one experiment he's done with students at Naropa frequently called, "The Walk." One takes a walk, comes back and then does writing using images of what one has seen. If you see a street sign or the name of a store, you may use that but you also use what those things remind you of—other places, other "sets," words out of dreams. If you see an elderly woman who reminds you of your great aunt Ruth, you flash on that and use it. You try to use all those things that come into your mind as material. It is a way of tuning up your mind, noticing what's in front of your nose rather than relying on what you feel and then make the associations. Another thing is going out and noticing all the red—a red hat, a red car, a red face. That's wonderful to do whether you're writing or not. It heightens your perceptions.

The marvelous poet Dick Gallup, who has taught at Naropa for a number of years, has very interesting ways of getting poems to happen: he'll suggest a poem where each line has a color in it or a season—and also working with forms. Some students work wonderfully with forms. They come here thinking they want to be experimental and get away from the sonnet or the haiku or whatever, and then their minds can do it best with some kind of gorgeous structure.

NB: I notice that you're doing a workshop in two days. Is there any pedagogical reason for making it that intense?

AW: I do want it intense. We'll do some very direct experiments in class and hopefully, they can also do one assignment that night which we will then pick up on and discuss the next day and then I'll try to meet with people individually later in the week. Diane di Prima has done eight-hour marathons and that idea of having writing extend the limits is interesting too—it's not something you stop doing for dinner or a coffee break. When you get on a writing binge, sometimes a poem will keep you going for twenty-four hours or more. And it's a challenge to follow your mind for that amount of time, quite extraordinary.

NB: Sound has turned out to be important to a number of people I've talked with, but you seem to have been conscious of its importance from a young age.

AW: I always was an avid reader and my parents were constant readers and had a good library and so on, but it was somehow hearing poetry out loud, reading it oneself out loud so that one can almost feel it physically, feel the vibration in the language. This is the effect too, of Mantra. It awakens parts of your body and brain. I had that experience, so that was something I was after in my work. Not all of my writing is geared that way, or consciously chant work, but it's important and natural to me. My own sound made me stronger.

The development of the reading scene or situation in this country the last ten years has been quite interesting. Many people I've spoken with say they have never had an experience of poetry until they've heard it read aloud and I think one can bring alive Shelley's poems or Shakespeare and Sappho by trying to present them orally. But I also think the boundaries between art performance and poetry are a little thin at times; one isn't quite sure: "Is it a poem or is it a performance? Where is it going and how much is the person presenting putting into it?" You might read it later yourself and it would be less powerful. I think some of my work is song and meant to be chanted. Others are as strong on the page.

Many students come to the Kerouac School obsessed with the idea of poetry being primarily oral and I have to make them pay attention to what they're doing on the page as well. In fact, one naturally loves the page. It's like an art work; the shape of the poem is exciting sitting in blank space and can conjure up all kinds of things. There are so many possibilities on the page that it doesn't have to get off the page to be experimental. There are things that haven't been done yet on the 8½ x 11 sheet of white typing paper. Many writers can present their work in an exciting, dynamic way, can get away with endlessly presenting *themselves* and be sloppy on the page. So there should be a happy balance. You have to have a text to spring forth from. There are some poets who don't read aloud. A poet like John Ashbery reads in a monotone, but he allows you to enter his language in an extraordinary way. I can't imagine having his poetry dramatically presented; it would be terrible, a strain.

NB: When Robert Bly read at Michigan State, he was dramatic.

AW: He is quite a showman. We read together in Rotterdam several years ago. He was up there with a dulcimer singing Yeats. Allen had been performing Blake with his harmonium. It seemed every poet had to get an instrument and their lineage poet to bring back to life. Joni Mitchell gave me a dulcimer once and said, "You should sing your poems." I couldn't get the two together. I enjoyed plucking on it and trying to sing with it, but I feel I have my innate music that I can't put to any instrument but my own vocal chords. I've worked with musicians and sometimes it's interesting and exciting, but the musicians have their stubborn ideas: "This is a jazz number," "This is country," or "This is blues." They'll try to get you to fit your work into these categories which aren't true to the poems; poems present new forms, new music, new tones. I'm trying now to work with musicians who are sensitive to the demands of the poem.

NB: You've said some things that suggest you see Buddhism as a way of encouraging a state of mind that is useful to writing.

AW: I think that's true. If you become a serious Buddhist, there are going to be periods when you are so involved with the practice, looking at your mind in ways you hadn't before, it could block or inhibit writing. It's like anything you delve into deeply: you can handle only that at the time. Writing for me has always been a practice and it's something that is with me all the time. I think Buddhism is a parallel practice. Buddhist practice should ideally infiltrate your whole life to make you a more awake, alert, functioning person and a saner being on the planet. You're not constantly motivated by your neurosis. A lot of experiments we do, especially with beginning students, are trying to reverse neurotic psychology, bring people into the moment, get them awake to what's in front of them, and cut the neurotic indulging aspect of being an artist. Your neurosis clouds your vision, so you "trip out" on things and your experience of them isn't true. One might say the best writing is by the craziest people. Of course, but in that moment of creation, the craziness is channeled or transmuted into something absolutely enlightening. Use your rage, use your jealousy, your passion, but put it out in front of you and don't be lost in it. Use those states skillfully.

In the Buddhist practice, when you look at your mind, you see your neurotic patterns. "Buddhism" isn't the best term because anyone can sit still. When you're doing sitting meditation, you aren't meditating on the eternal flame or the white light; it's looking at your mind, and what comes up. The fantasies, the emotions, the projections, etc. You see them and you say, "Those are just thoughts" and you let them go. Craziness comes from having those thoughts become solidified so that you might think you're John Lennon and go kill the other John Lennon or whatever. That is an extreme example, of course.

At the root of the Buddhist practice is the likelihood that you'll make friends with yourself: you look at your mind and stop playing games. It cuts a lot of those patterns where you're trying to put one over on others and consequently, yourself. When you see your ego is an alien parasite feeding on you, you can work on it, transmute it. You can see how slippery it is and how manipulative and how it controls your thinking, your actions so much of the time. You can look at poems and see what the writer's mind is like; you wouldn't have to know anything else about them. It's remarkable.

When you sit in front of the typewriter and a blank white page, anything is possible. It's so refreshing when you come to that in a sane way. Not all the time. I will certainly come to it anxiety ridden because I haven't written a poem in so long, or the poem I want to write is not coming out right. I find my life is saner with having my poetry be a practice and not worrying about my next book—the maintaining of my identity as a poet, etc.

What's been nice about the poetry world has been the tremendous support one gets among one's male and female confreres. The stakes are low in poetry; it's not like the art world, for example. There you might make a great deal of money on your work; poems aren't marketable art objects. No one is going to pay thousands of dollars for a piece of paper; maybe when you've been dead hundreds of years and it's handwritten in indelible ink. (*Laughter.*)

NB: Someone said the difference between academics and writers is that academics like repetition, while writers want to try new things all the time.

AW: Right. I try to do all the experiments with the class. I'm as much a student as they are. That's the only way I can continue to teach. I've been teaching Gertrude Stein a great deal and have notes and so forth, but there's always this desire to make the material new.

NB: A lot of the women I've talked to have had trouble doing their own work . . .

AW: When they're teaching. It comes and goes. I find when I'm teaching in a writing class, I'm inspired to do more work. Some of my best work has come out of a Naropa poetics assignment.

NB: Are you saying that the things you do in class . . .

AW: Turn into real poems, work that I accept; it's not simply some exercise tossed off for the sake of this class. Real work. I did a Stein class one summer and some of the poets were involved with demonstrating at the Rocky Flats plutonium plant, and so that reality was entering into the class. Many of the protestors were arrested and everything had a mysterious Steinesque quality. It was like a scenario for some play of hers: the flatness—how in her work everything has equal weight and there is no beginning, middle, end. It's very hot, and flat out there with the hills in the distance, demonstrating and being arrested, being put into this bus, waiting endlessly in the sun, the policemen with their megaphones repeating the same thing. It's like a Stein work with its repetitions. I always think her writing resembles riding in a plane and seeing things from a marvelous objective distance. There's an interesting objectivity in her; there is this emotional relationship but it's not expressed in characters or experiences: everything becomes flatted out—democratic. I was writing a poem, not really sleeping very much, and then I would come in and present the poem I was doing and the notes for the class that day and we would read some of her works. My notes and the poem became one big work. I've been going back and looking at it and I'm seeing it as a piece of writing, so I'm going to try to make a book of it. It's called "Loom Down the Thorough Narrow"—from a line of hers. But I was able to integrate my life into that class and also be writing this ongoing poem. I was also using my own dream and journal entries and other details of living in Colorado. It was also the summer that St. Mark's Church had a terrible fire and getting that news when I was in Colorado was hard for me ... It was very upsetting not to be able to do anything. So that entered the poem as well. It was one of the most successful classes because I was so involved in making something myself.

But there are periods ... Right now, I'm just learning to do my work with a baby in my life. I wanted this baby terribly, I'm in ecstasy. Actually, recently, the baby is turning into a muse for the poems.

NB: You said, "At school I was reading the classics, had a solid education, but if I let the masters take over—one would give up if you had to compare yourself with Yeats, Rilke, Shakespeare—especially a young student female poet!" It sounds like being a woman is freeing.

AW: In the middle of one long night, I realized the women right now could seize the artistic power or energy, as poets. Most of my teachers have been male and the poets I've gotten much from have been male; I think I came at this lucky time when the male poets who were my peers were able to transmit their knowledge in a way that they weren't doing ten years earlier. Diane di Prima once talked about how so many of the talented women that she knew in the so-called Beat scene were destroyed. They were not given the technical information or the sources or the lineage, so they dried up, committed suicide, destroyed themselves out of frustration—one thing or another. Diane, of course, was a fighter and survivor. She has always been an inspiration to me. She's a tough woman, not personally, but in terms of her commitment to her work.

I've been very lucky. It's hard in the beginning: you have doubts and often men seem to be deciding your fate. But I do feel I'm on the crest of a new wave of exciting women writers.

THEODORE WEISS

NB: I want to ask you about your poem, "Into Summer," where you talk about your students' passivity. I'm curious about these lines:

But now each must heed the music
mumbling in him—in some crazy way
on top of the brown, green sticks out,
and a whitish, tiny kind of flower—
that strange blend of the burnt
and the growing.

TW: It's a poem which has a considerable background and I was perhaps too careful not to make much of it. The poem was written while all the burning was going on: the burning of books, the burning of people. I was living at Bard and every day I would walk to school past two fields. One morning they burned the weed-choked fields down rather than take the time to cut the weeds. Dismayed by all that scorching, I was reminded of what was going on in Germany and Russia.

I went to class, and my students, there they were, most of them slumped into themselves a little like those burnt fields, and I wondered, "Is this everywhere?" But then as I came back another day, through all that seeming death, new things were beginning to stir again and so that poem. The hope was that the human creature, if he survives, make something of himself despite all the horrible destructiveness. That's been a permanent theme of mine. That's why a later book, later than the one in which that poem appears, is called *Fireweeds.* That's why it says the burnt land will be green.

157

*NB: What does "each must heed the music mumbling in him"
mean?*

TW: I think if there isn't music in us all, there is music in none of
us. Poetry is for all of us, even though a lot of us are stunted or our
ears are stuffed to our own voices as well as other voices. The music
trying to find its way out of us is the fundamental impulse which
makes us human.

*NB: You said in your letter that your teaching and your writing feed
each other and the examples you gave suggested to me that the influence is very direct.*

TW: My teaching background is a little unusual for most writers
today. Until coming here, I taught only literature courses: at Chapel
Hill, at Yale. At Yale, I was assigned a writing course, but I was told
not to allow the students in it to do creative writing. When I got to
Bard College, by nature of the program, so-called progressive education, I taught almost anything in literature that I wished. That's the
closest I came to giving myself an education because I had three
classes and twelve advisees pursuing their own separate courses. So
at any one time I had fifteen, sixteen courses and I read madly in all
directions. That was exhilarating. I was literally—and literarily—
high most of the time; I felt I was jumping from one trapeze to
another. One hour I might be talking about the metaphysical poets,
the next hour, the Elizabethan playwrights, then twentieth-century
poetry or the Russian novel.

    Anything was possible. We had what we called senior projects,
and one bright young man wanted to do a study of *The Tale of Genji.*
I liked him and I was intrigued by the idea, so I said if it was accepted
I would oversee it. Well, I read the whole *Genji* and it was fascinating. Bard College was, in other words, a place that encouraged one
to explore oneself as well as literature. Though the arts were im-
mensely important at Bard and many students were writing, I taught
writing only to individuals in tutorial. I never taught a workshop,
and only coming here, to Princeton, a more conservative place, have
I found a good part of my work is teaching the writing of poetry. At
the same time, I'm in the English Department; so even here I'm not
exclusively occupied with student writing but with realized writing
as well, and that makes a difference. I don't know that I'd enjoy what

many poets are now up to, that is, concentrating exclusively on student writing. Whatever its immediacy, that's likely to be a little thin, even if the students are gifted.

I'm always a little skeptical about teaching writing until I do it. Everyone says, "You can't teach people to write, can you?" I say, "No, but you can teach them to rewrite." It's exciting to see the first stirrings and you teach them something about what writing is; so whether or not they excel or become full-fledged writers is by the way. We in the Princeton writing program are not so arrogant as to pretend to be able to produce poets, but we are hopeful that we can make good readers; for a good course in writing draws students into the presence of poetry in a way that a regular English literature course can't. In a workshop students get as close to the actualities of writing as anyone can get and that is very valuable. I used to say —thank goodness there's not any danger of it—if I were head of an English department, I would require all freshmen, all English majors at least, to take a term of creative writing; not to make them poets, necessarily, but to get them up against it so they can see the difficulties, the astonishment of a good poem.

NB: Is your work shaped by the literature you're teaching at the time? I wondered why you mentioned a connection between teaching Shakespeare and your poem "Caliban Remembers" in your letter.

TW: Shakespeare's been an addiction. I very early contracted the happy disease. It's not something I pick up . . .

NB: And put into a poem?

TW: Oh, no. On occasion I will, but not usually. The plays are in my blood now, filled with all my Shakespearian work. Critics on occasion accuse me of being literary which is a little absurd because I am. *(Laughter.)* What do they expect of someone who has spent a good part of his life teaching literature? I would go so far as to say that most writers today are very conscious of literature and their part in it. Whether they like it or not, they are to varying degrees literary. Americans used to be proud of their unique, virginal state which usually meant pretty raw stuff; but since Eliot and Pound, that's nonsense. Though some writers still pretend to be part of the great unwashed, or rough and tumble, if you look closely at the best of them, you'll see all the reading which lies behind their poems.

Years ago when writing verse became serious to me, I too felt I had to be American in what I was doing and I tried for a while to write straight—I was about to say "crooked"—but I soon began to feel that it was a lie. But maybe it was foolish of me to acknowledge my sources. Being at Princeton marks me. Some people tend to be suspicious. It's elitist and that's not good; so they automatically assume I must be a certain kind of person. An article about my work that came out in *Parnassus* some time ago was an interesting, lively piece, but the critic made a considerable to-do about my literary background and she said, with what seemed like surprise, that she had to admit that she not only found it genuine and necessary, but likeable.

It's an old problem. We understandably, sensibly, want our writers to be fresh, immediate, in touch with experience rather than with books, and I well realize that books are not a substitute for living; but they are a genuine part of any cultivated life and to deny their presence in one's life seems deceitful. Emerson was one of the first Americans to make this big to-do against the literary. A lot of the Romantics did; Wordsworth with, "Don't go to books, go to nature." Of course, most of them were exploring and taking inspiration from books all the time they were saying one must take nature straight. This is a fixed American idea, though, as I've suggested, it has its roots in England as well. Critics used to say Milton was second hand and Shakespeare was original. This is bunk. Not too long ago, working on *Hamlet* in class, I pointed out how bookish this play is. Everywhere someone is either reading a book or talking about writing books. It's most striking how preoccupied the young Shakespeare was with the act of writing, the place of writing, the nature of writing, and books that mattered to him. Yet surely it's not surprising in a young, ambitious, enormously gifted writer, determined to make his way.

On the other hand, I don't agree with Bloom who insists that all books are the children of books. To some degree that's true: we're all shaped by the literature we've read. But I think there's a difference between poets who are lively and urgent and those who are truly academic types. You don't even have to read books to be an academic type. I remember how amused I was when the Beats first exploded on the scene. A lot of poets who had been New Critical types wrote very complicated New Critical poems. However, since they were followers rather than leaders, when the Beats came along, they gravitated to them and their manner of writing. If one looked closely at their poems, they were just as dull, sheepish and fashionable as their New Critical poems. It's not really a matter of whether you lean on books or don't lean on books; it's a matter of how hard you lean on anything. The passion or the intensity or the concentration is what matters.

NB: Do you encourage your students to read a lot?

TW: Oh, yes.

NB: Do you require them to read?

TW: It varies and depends on what state they're in. With the young ones I do; with the more advanced ones, I'm usually satisfied to throw out suggestions, ones made as strongly as I can. Eliot was right: a poet needs to know what's been there; so I urge on my students major figures both for themselves and because they illustrate the basic qualities a good poet ought to know about and have. And this seems to work fairly well.

NB: Would you be willing to name some of them?

TW: I often start with Blake. Then I go to Hopkins. I like them to see an immediate poet, a passionate poet like Blake; then a passionately technical one like Hopkins. And to see how their passions meet. Then I move to the moderns: I give them Williams and if time allows, some Yeats and Pound. I'd like them to see how much there is to learn and what variety of approaches and emphases exist.

NB: I like your poetry best when it captures those moments of elation.

TW: That puts pretty well something I've been after. One of the things that has preoccupied me is how you make long poems out of such moments. It's almost a contradiction in terms. How you turn a lyric impulse into a dramatic, large work is a fantastic challenge, but it has occupied me all my writing life. I suppose it means in one sense trying to expand the lyric incredibly. That's why Wordsworth was very important to me, especially with such a poem as "Tintern Abbey" which is enlarged by the meditative, by views of the past and things to come and by recollections of his childhood. Though he locates the poem very precisely in one place, it's the voluminousness of the poem, what he can suck up in that one place, that makes it so attractive to me. Aeschylus was very important to me because, aside from other things, his drama is, as some critics, hard put to describe it, resorting to a kind of contradiction, have called it, "static drama." "Static drama" sounds mad except that, in what plays of his remain, we usually have a static figure like Prometheus who centralizes the action. Things come to him: the winds come, the messenger comes; but all of it focuses in and derives from him, so that, in a sense, this is monologic drama. This intrigued me endlessly and seemed to relate to Browning's monologues. I've tried very hard to develop and master a poem which is an expanded monologue. Years ago I wrote a long single poem called *Gunsight* which was an attempt to find all the voices in my voice.

In each of us are different characters waiting their moment on stage: a thief, wretch, intelligent person. We're made up of all these complicated and contradictory moments, and in that long, would-be dramatic piece, I tried to find a situation in which all the voices would have their opportunity to break out at their time in the play. So it's been a long search for situations in which, given our lyrical fix, one can still find resources in oneself and one's material that exceed ordinary limits. I've chafed at limitations. We have so much we never use in language. So I do find the momentary work of the lyrical mode pleasurable, but not altogether satisfactory. I prefer the long sojourn a long poem requires and affords.

NB: Your poems are wonderfully complicated. I had the feeling I could read them over and over and keep finding things in them.

TW: Well, that's encouraging. I have wanted a very rich web of things. It's a complicated world we live in. I have wanted to give everything its chance. Such an approach is dangerous because you may overburden the poem, but every method of writing has its risks.

NB: How do you handle these issues with your students? I would imagine that they tend to build rather narrow poems.

TW: Yes. Most of my students are not equal to this attitude and I don't push it on them. But perhaps I should make more of it than I do as a goal. I do require them to try their hand at a sequence. I believe that you can get them to recognize change of pace, modulation. One of the problems in modern poetry is that there's been an almost mystical enthusiasm for finding one's voice. Often you have poets who have a voice but with very little in it. I tell my students that their voice is important for what it has to say and that, in all likelihood, if they are serious writers, their voices will take care of themselves.

Too many poets have been so worried about their personal stand that they've forgotten there are larger things to worry about: the worlds outside the world inside, finding those and voicing those; so I encourage students to enrich their reach in poetry by a larger range of interest. One of the problems with young writers is that they don't know what they're interested in or what might be interesting in them. You have to help them find their interests. Also, many of them, and not just the young, are fairly narcissistic. It's important to make them realize that there's a world out there that deserves attention and will enrich them and their readers. It may even deepen their insides. So I use all kinds of poets who seem to me to illustrate this: poets who know they're worthwhile as their worlds are. They do not put a special premium on themselves to the exclusion of other things. They put a premium on themselves, if they do, as a consequence of and for what they've been able to appreciate and absorb. The old statement that you find yourself by losing yourself is one that our age has lost sight of altogether.

So the whole nonsense about an identity crisis: it's true there's an identity crisis if you're not interested in anything. If you're deeply interested in anything, you don't think about the crisis. You are too busy, too occupied, for it. It's only the concern of the unemployed or the unoccupied or the vain. One thing I've never thought much about except as people stress it: "What is my voice?" I don't much care. I say to my students, "Be careful not to get your voice, even if you can, too soon because then you're likely to get locked into it. Try to keep open as long as you can. Sooner or later we all close down to being rather limited, obvious individuals."

NB: But your poem "An Everlasting Once" seems to praise a man who goes off by himself to write poetry.

TW: He was a heroic figure in my mind, a version of the isolated, modern artist. I originally had in mind a Blakean young man with luminous, powerful gifts, gifts burdensome for their richness, who thinks he will change all, not only the literary world, the human world. He has great designs for himself, but he finds to his astonishment, as he goes on, that the world refuses to recognize him. He is too large, too much, too insistent. Thus he becomes more and more private, turns inward altogether. As he grows into his prophetic works, they become more and more worlds unto themselves as though he, finally, knowing he cannot in his own work, in his own world, in his own time, change the world, turns himself into his work and makes that a great world of its own, he still hoping, I suppose, that eventually it will renovate the world, or help it to see things as they are.

I was struck by this kind of figure who is rebuffed in his own time or, worse, ignored; what desperate strategems he has to resort to. There are many such artists: Hopkins, Emily Dickinson, Walt Whitman—though he pretended otherwise—writers, painters. They have to become their whole world; they not only have to become writers, but their readers, their audience, their own company, and everything else. And it is very much an American phenomenon. Blake was not an American, though he had Americanic powers, passions and idealisms. But the poem to a degree minimizes that other sense I have of the importance of a man's belonging to and being part of tradition. That's the troubling thing about being American. Whether we like it or not, we are part of a large world just by the fact that the whole world elsewhere has flowed into America; name a race that hasn't become part of it. At the same time, Americans have been so proud of their uniqueness, their being absolutely original, and all that nonsense, that they have wanted to push away all sense of belonging. And in doing this, they've often required their poets to be that way (because they've ignored them!): Whitman, Dickinson. Williams felt this for years until he became famous in his sixties; so did Pound who battered away at America in Europe most of his life. So there is an essential, necessary contradiction at work in that poem as there is in me.

That poem is also curious because I draw on something quite outside my own world to furnish it, and that is Leningrad, the seige of it. But you know how far afield an artist may have to go to illustrate some truths! I read and saw what incredible heroism was required of people during the time of the seige by the Nazis. They got to the point where many of them burned their prize possessions to survive, and a large number, having devoured what was available, starved to death. I drew on that in the poem to suggest the sense in which we're always beseiged. We may have to resort in our life and work to measures as desperate as those the world imposes on us. But then the poem emphasizes again the little green coming up with a flower out of the burning, how the artist does make something out of his difficulties so that it persists even though the world has ignored it. In the end he, his work, is the growing stream, the undeniable mainstream. Literary historians talk of the mainstream and how this figure or that is merely a tributary or deflection. The poem's figure was ignored and wouldn't seem to be in it at all. But all the time, without the world's knowing or wanting to know, he was attending to cleaning and strengthening the mainstream.

NB: You've commented that when you started writing there were no workshops to encourage the young apprentice. Do you wish that you had gone to a workshop?

TW: The only person who was any use to me directly was Mark Van Doren at Columbia. And this was for his teaching, his attitude toward literature, rather than for any direct help. I would show him poems occasionally, but he would never say anything more than "Very interesting," or he would chuckle over an image. There was no attempt at criticism. Once I asked him about a poem I was working on, whether it should be in free verse or formal verse. And he said, "I wouldn't worry about that." But that was the kind of man he was, imperturbable—imperturbable for others. *(Laughter.)*

It's not so much that I regret there weren't workshops, but I do and did regret that there weren't others to share with because writing is a very lonely business, as everyone knows; one yearns for people who might give one an interested and intelligent, not to say critical, hearing. After all, we need to be informed by others. We need mirrors, especially thoughtful, reactive mirrors who don't merely reflect, but also show you what you can't see well. And I did regret that as a student I had very little. My students now have maybe too much of that.

The *Quarterly Review of Literature* has been very important to me in being a lifeline to other writers, seeing their work, writing to them, receiving letters from them; the exchange has been very wonderful. It has been a setting up of a community at a distance, with all kinds of people: we had a great deal of correspondence with Williams, Wallace Stevens, Rexroth. These were fundamentally important to us. And now it's exciting for us to read the work of young writers and try to understand what's happening. It keeps us in touch with newer things, and we do our best to read the poems so that we can, having tuned in on their particular music, if it seems necessary, suggest revisions.

NB   One of your poems about William Carlos Williams, "Yes, But . . ." seemed to imply a number of things about writers:

Only now I begin to understand
the doubts necessary to one
always open, always desperate
(his work's honesty, spontaneity—
work nothing, life—depended
on it),
        one too so given
over to the moment, so lover-
faithfully serving it,
He could remember or believe
in little else.

I saw a lot there. One is that the spontaneity and honesty in his poetry were not poses.

TW: Yes, that was the kind of man he was: very spontaneous; that very American man: very quick to respond, very quick to notice. His temperament and his way of life required that. Being a terribly busy doctor, busy night and day, he had to learn to attend to all his moments quickly. What was valuable to me was my sense of his availability to living, his openness, his taking in of life in a way that most of us don't.

NB: My sense is that writers tend to do that.

TW: Oh, of course. That's part of being a writer, although some of us, I guess, are sunk in ourselves. You remember Keats' wonderful distinction between Wordsworth and Shakespeare; Wordsworth, he said, was a poet primarily occupied with the world within himself. Shakespeare was so enamored of the world that we hardly know who Shakespeare was. There are those who say he never existed. *(Laughter.)* Well, that's as it should be with a major poet. Who is Homer? There's a voice, a huge colorful, all-inclusive voice in the work; but it's not personal in the way we usually think of personal.

NB: But you also say Williams was uncertain and you use the word "desperate."

TW: Yes. I used "desperate" because if you open yourself, you are at the mercy of what may go on. One reason so many people are closed up is they don't want to be hurt. If you're a feelingful, exposed person, since the world is not made to be kind, in many circumstances you may be very badly bruised. Again Keats, in that letter, admired Shakespeare because he could stand out in the open without seizing on some established religion or philosophy. And I find a certain amount of that in Williams.

NB: What did you mean by the statement that "the fool in us is sometimes the deepest, truest part, most worth listening to"?

TW: Shakespeare's fools are among his most extraordinary characters. I suppose the most impressive is Lear's fool who in a way brings him to reality. And I would say, though I say it with some hesitation because one has to recognize that the word "fool," as I use it here, is not concerned with "foolish," Williams was a fool. Now with Shakespeare's fool in *Lear,* one has a sense of a hurt creature who has possibly been damaged by life. I'm going back to my fireweeds. Therefore, he is sprung open and is available willy-nilly to what in life is convivial, but he is not capable of the larger direct confrontations. He hasn't, for instance, Lear's strength which makes it possible for Lear to persist through the play's whole long period, to survive most of its rigors. Yet, at the same time, the fool in us may make us available to currents in ourselves, that inner music which we otherwise may not hear. I'm not the enemy of sanity, God knows, but I am the enemy of habituation which covers this over, and modern sanity tends to be a tight, orderly, routine habituation and that's dangerous.

NB: In the introduction to your Shakespeare book you also say that one of your themes is going to be the importance of play.

TW: That's exactly what Shakespeare illustrates very often. His characters, a number of them, are so full of vitality that no matter how large their roles, they are wanting to play additional parts, whether it be that very fundamental Bottom in *A Midsummer Night's Dream* who's not satisfied to be just Bottom; he wants to play all the parts. This almost ruthless appetite for living would do it all: I want to be this person and that and that and that. Or a character so full of life, he or she, a Cleopatra, can throw the world away; even the world isn't large enough or tuned in, like them, on the infinite variety that exists within them. And Shakespeare, at the same time, is always moving towards song and dance because those are the two moments in which the human race is most free. Song is a self-sufficient thing. So is dance. When you dance, you don't go anywhere except to where you really are. When you sing, you don't use your breath to buy something, to urge something, to persuade something; you use it for your own and the moment's fulfillment. And so in his plays.

NB: Does that idea influence your teaching at all? Do you try to get your students to play with different forms?

TW: Yes I do, although modern students are wary of forms. You have to work hard on them to get them to write sonnets or villanelles. Their unpreparedness and their innocence as well as the practice of their recent great predecessors make them suspicious of all this; and unless a poet is very capable, it is true that the forms can become straight-jackets. Unless a person is almost born to these forms and unless he's exceptionally adroit, there is a problem with writing sonnets, say. I had one student who had developed a way of dealing with language and the world that was very fresh; her poems would often actually become poems. And she was bright enough to say to me one day that she was beginning to be dissatisfied with this, the limitations of it, and would like to try something else. I said, "Good for you. How about writing sonnets?" So for months she tried to write them and she could hardly write one. Finally she got to the point where she could turn out ten lines and then she'd falter; but gradually she did turn out a fairly workmanlike sonnet. But it had the earmarks of earlier sonnets, and you could feel her working at it, not making enough of her own out of it. But I do think it was a good experience for her.

NB: Do you do anything else to encourage your students to break out of patterns?

TW: As a teacher, I have tried not to interfere too much. I've thought about this a great deal. I try to invite them, encourage them, and when I see what they have, I work to improve and expand that; not to give them things, but to find the things they have: that's the best gift after all. But there are certain awarenesses which one does well to try to drive home.

NB: On the other hand, there's what you've said and what Marvin Bell has said in a couple of places: the best way to get the unconscious up is to ignore it.

TW: Yes. That's right. There's no point in worrying about these things. If one is really passionately committed or engaged, all kinds of things come up. Oh those blessed moments when we go beyond ourselves rather than being busy seeking ourselves.

NB: In an interview you said that "when the mind begins to ignite, everything becomes the right fuel ... whether it is some magnetic attraction, or it is that the mind has reached such a high pitch of accomplishment that it can make everything seem right." Does that refer to what we were just talking about?

TW: Yes, I think so.

NB: You just begin working and then ...

TW: Yes, and the mind tunes in on itself and on everything else. I've known it best in long poems. Short poems are a momentary tuning in until static comes, but in long poems, if you can find a way into them ... I worked on the poem *Gunsight* many, many years intermittently, and one summer I finally decided I had to finish it when we were in Rome. We were living near the Pantheon and buses and motorcycles were roaring through, and the poem is a war poem, so it seemed right, somehow. And I had a strong sense of the whole poem. I can remember very well how it began to go. Everything seemed to be necessary, to sweep in, even those buses and vespas! I seemed to be central of a great telephone system to the universe and everything was touching me, flowing through me. Mad, hallucinatory, but wonderful.

In the latest long poem that I've written, *Recoveries,* published twenty years after *Gunsight,* some of the same sustained and sustaining pleasures came my way, a world that day by day—and informing sleepless and sleeping nights as well—went on developing. Amusingly enough, if *Gunsight* was a distinctly American, American-set poem finished in Italy, *Recoveries* is a poem about a Florentine fresco written mainly in Princeton, even though it did gestate in many places from Israel and Hungary to Yaddo. And one of its prime promptings was the extraordinary moment when for the first time— and maybe the last—some frescoes traveled to the United States and the Metropolitan Museum in New York where I saw them. Off I went on another long trip of composing; mad, hallucinatory, but wonderful.

NB: Do you have any idea how that happens?

TW: It happens only through two things: sheer effort and sheer good luck. The mountains—or the frescoes—move to Mohammed! As though the world actually bestirs itself to inspire, to help us. But we have to be ready—primed—for that help.

NB: Like in the poem about the student who's trying to write about the weeds?

TW: Yes, a very early one, "Preface."

NB: There it seems to be a matter of just keeping at it.

TW: Until you get it. Sometimes if you work hard enough and if you're lucky, the work begins to attract things and the way becomes sweet. The way flies will go to honey, something begins to find all that concentration interesting as though some muse begins to wonder, "What's going on here?" *(Laughter.)* If you get up enough energy and imagination, you magnetize and draw things into your center. But it does take immense amounts of power. I find that one of the fascinating things about writing. It takes that dynamic center: you don't write well out of anemia.

RICHARD WILBUR

NB: You said that "Birches" "is happy in all the ways in which a poem can be happy" because it "does justice to world, to self, to literary tradition, and to a culture." What do your poetry students have the most trouble doing justice to?

RW: Like all young people, they are better at doing justice to self than to the world. I don't know whether you *can* do justice to your self without doing justice to the world, but in any case there's a lot of self-absorption among young people and, most of the time, what one is doing in writing courses is pointing out moments of self-absorption. I have all my students get involved in the act of criticism. We present the poem of some student anonymously—twelve or thirteen copies, so that everyone can be staring at it—and everybody talks and *always,* unless it's the utterly successful poem which disarms criticism, *always* somebody says, "What were you trying to say in line six?" And the writer answers, in effect, "I did say it." And then the original critic, backed by perhaps two or three others now, says, "No, you didn't say it. No, it didn't come through to us. You were nudging your closest friend, maybe, but you weren't conveying it to the general reader." I suppose that's the most valuable thing that gets done in a half year of writing-teaching: people come to learn that they have to go to extraordinary lengths to compel a trained and willing reader to see something of what they want to show, think something of what they want thought. I remember Allen Tate saying in *The House of Fiction* that the commonest failing in the writing of amateur fiction could be called the "unwritten story." People think they have told the story; they haven't, they simply haven't told it.

171

The love of small vocabulary and incoherence that accompanied the sixties has made it harder for young writers now, even though everyone is trying to recover from that. You remember that expression, "You know, you know, you know"? It seems to me that that expression was not just a tic, but a demand for reassurance that one belonged. "We understand each other without speaking, don't we?" I think that's what "you know" meant a lot of the time: "Aren't we all trustworthy and don't we all share the same likes and dislikes?" There was something conspiratorial or something of the shibboleth about "you know."

I think the students of the "Cambodian incursion" days were making a gesture of solidarity through that expression: affirming their mistrust of words and their respect for mute communion. Nowadays you can almost see bright people struggling to reinvent the complex sentence before your eyes. A friend of mine who is a college administrator every now and then has to say a complex sentence, and he will get into one of those morasses that begins, "I would hope that we would be able . . . " He never talked that way when I first met him, but even at his age, at his distance from the crisis in the lives of younger people, he's been to some extent alienated from easy speech.

All of this is reflected in writing courses and in a feeling among the students that it would be embarrassing to be too eloquent, too literary, too clear. It wouldn't be honest, in a certain debased sense of that word, because it would be showy. I suppose all of that is distilled in the familiar expression, "You talk like a book." *(Laughter.)* You'd think that it would or could be a compliment, but it never is. *(Laughter.)*

NB: One person I talked to said that he'd been accused of being literary. He thought that was a strange thing to accuse a poet of, but he had to agree he was.

RW: Yes. *(Laughter.)* I suppose poetry has become in good part sub-literary nowadays, and so one can understand very sharply what was meant by that man's critic. A number of years ago, the poem began to be confused with the rock lyric *(laughter)* by a great many people. And that meant shapelessness and want of grammar and any old kind of rhyming if one rhymed at all.

NB: Do you attempt to correct that attitude when you teach?

RW: I'm not very coersive; I guess I'm going to get more coersive this fall. It is, after all, 1981. I do want to encourage my students, not necessarily to understand scansion theoretically, but to try their hands, at least once, at some simple formal structure. There are always several people, sometimes more that, who want to work in meters. I'm not complaining bitterly, but I think that I shouldn't let anybody get through the semester without brushing with that kind of discipline. I have in the past allowed people simply to try to do well in the manner that came easiest to them. And I can't explain why I'm now going to be a little more authoritarian, but I am. *(Laughter.)* I guess I'm just fed up. *(Laughter.)* I'm damned if I'm going to let any of my writing students be utterly ignorant of the literature of the past, or their work be utterly irrelevant to it.

NB: Do you give your writing students reading assignments?

RW: I pick different books in different years, sometimes an anthology containing a good deal of work from the past; but, in any case, I keep presenting them with mimeographed poems of the past and asking them to read in all ages and in as many languages as they can manage. To further that a little, I'll give them an exercise in translation: a French poem, accompanied by a literal translation and by a critical commentary borrowed from somebody, all of this to be worked up into a translation. I've even asked people to translate from less familiar languages because, with a sufficient amount of apparatus, I think it can be done. If the right sounds are made aloud, somehow that's a penetration of the poem's spirit. If they hear what kind of meter it is, that helps too.

I do think that there's a swing back now toward some sort of core curriculum, and so students are more and more picking up a sense of literary tradition. The period of disruption caused by the Vietnam War was disastrous in that respect. At many places I knew of, and at Wesleyan where I was teaching, many students got the idea that the past was indeed dead and that all they needed to learn was themselves. Oh, of course, they needed to learn also the things which they had appropriated to themselves, or decorated themselves with, such as William Blake and Hermann Hesse; there were certain things you were expected to have in your pocket, as you had a guitar in your hand during that period. *(Laughter.)* But I was most annoyed by the teachers who went along with it all and, indeed, fostered a great deal of it, told students that the past was irrelevant, accepted that nonsense word "relevance" as a way of acquitting students of making the acquaintance of humanity throughout its whole temporal range. Such a primitive notion: that you can ignore the past as a mob of strangers. Those people represent what one might again be, or what one still is. At Smith, a lot of my present students are pretty decently trained in the literary tradition. There are outstanding girls who really know it. Everybody has some sense of it, and you don't need to bully people into reading Chaucer; they will have read some Chaucer.

NB: You have said that it's hard to be a poet in a culture with no strong sense of community. Do you still believe that?

RW: For Americans, it's a problem. A country like France, for a contrast, feels itself to be monolithic, is violently conscious of its own culture and its own past and has one big cultural and governmental center. We're spread all over the place. That's good in a way; I'm not kicking about that, but we are. Los Angeles and Boston are remote from each other in more ways than one, and surely it's good for every place to have its own character; but when one begins to think about the country, one has to think of something fragmented or incoherent; as Brooks Adams said, "The incoherence of American democracy." He thought America would have been more coherent in every sense if George Washington's notion of extending a canal from Washington to the Ohio had been put into action. That, he thought, would have made Washington not only the governmental, but also the commerical and the cultural center of the country.

NB: Your poems are very rich, but you sometimes wait a long time for them. Could you wait that long when you were twenty?

RW: Oh, yes. Yes, I did. I suppose I wrote a little faster than I write now, but I've always written very, very slowly and that's one reason there tends to be, for better or for worse, quite a lot in the individual line, why paraphrase would be hard. If you picked up the latest issue of the average poetry periodical nowadays, you'd find for the most part a density of language which is approximately that of prose. It is sometimes good in an affectingly sincere way, but because I'm a product of my time, it lacks for me the excitement that I look for in poetry. I look for the unparaphrasable; too many poems are now being written which are their own paraphrases.

NB: Can you persuade your students to wait the way you do?

RW: It's hard and unfair, isn't it, to do a thing like that, because part of my job is to bully them into writing eight poems and seven exercises in a semester. So I must keep the pressure on them. At the same time, I have to be understanding of blocks, because I would surely have a block if I were placed under my own demands. I do talk about how too bad it is to spoil a good idea by executing it too rapidly. And I do as my students do in our group critiques; point out that such and such a line is pretty flat compared to the rest; but I think that's as far as I go with that kind of thing.

NB: Some people say that their writing students come into class believing that the most important aspect of a poem or story is its theme and that they have to think up something significant to say before they begin to write.

RW: I can recall student poems which seemed not to have arisen from the genuine concerns of the poet but simply from an effort to sound weighty. One student, way back there when I was first teaching at Harvard, said to me, "Mr. Wilbur, you're not an easy person to write for." And I said, "Great God, have you been writing for me all this semester?" I guess that many people do come into your class with the feeling that they are to some extent writing for you, and if they think that the English teacher wants them to adopt a theme of proven weight, there it comes: a poem which has been misconceived from the start. I often quote to my students that well-known bit of Auden's where he says that the most promising thing in a young writer is a hankering to play around with words, and that the most unpromising thing to hear from a young writer is, "I have lot of ideas I want to express." *(Laughter.)*

NB: But you don't have any system for handling that.

RW: No. I think that if I ever say anything about the matter in class, I do so in the particular case. I might say, "We know by now that this writer is capable of something better than this. This appears to be a high-minded propaganda poem, or a poem on a supposedly obligatory weighty theme, and that's why it isn't any good." Not that one shouldn't start with some sense of a subject, but one shouldn't start with somebody else's subject.

NB: Do you regularly teach literature?

RW: I've always taught literature. In fact, I started out to be a teacher of literature; at any rate, that's what chiefly interested me when I was at Harvard. I really wouldn't enjoy teaching, if I were teaching only creative writing. I *like* teaching writing as a relaxation from the other kind of teaching, as another kind of relationship with the students—inevitably, a more personal one—and another way of connecting the literature of the past which interests me with the present.

NB: Most of the literature classes I had emphasized what you call "paraphrasable meaning," but I imagine that you focus on something else. What do you do in your literature classes?

RW: When I teach Milton, for example, I deal with him in all respects, spending a lot of time on matters of technique. You have to with a great technician, with the greatest verse architect in history; you cannot understand that "L'Allegro" and "Il Penseroso" are serious poems unless you worry the structure to death and discover the ideas implicit in the structure. And so I and the students wrestle for several days until we've found the structure of the two poems. You have to talk about theology too and to some extent, history. I've always been inclined to slack on that latter side of things because when I was in college, the New Criticism had just come along vivifying the reading process, but making some things impermissible. Biographical and historical information were considered dispensable at that time, and so if there's something I badly neglect, it's those two things. When I teach Poe, I'm always resistant to biographical interpretations of his stories, although Poe gives his own birthdate to William Wilson and the tales contain all kinds of sly references to his life. I probably have a certain culpable blindness to the pertinence of biography.

NB: Do you read aloud in class?

RW: I do that a great deal, both when I'm teaching literature and when I'm teaching writing. I think there's no substitute for it. You read something aloud as well as you can, and I think you thereby give a new sense of its measure as well as of its meaning. If you're reading a student poem aloud to your students, they all know that you're going to do as well by it as you can. And if it doesn't quite work, they have a fresh sense of where and why it doesn't work. I read things as long as "Lycidas" aloud to my classes when I'm teaching literature; the musical and emotional dimensions can't be got in any better way, and also a feeling of the poem as a whole. If one is talking at it and explicating little corners of it, one can lose what they call "the big picture"; one can simplify wonderfully by reading. I try to get students to read aloud too, a thing they're often scared to do because they haven't been asked to do it in any primary or secondary school. I wish that that were done more in the earlier stages of schooling; everyone should have a competence in that.

NB: How did you happen to write on Poe, or to write criticism at all?

RW: The thing that excited me most as an undergraduate at Amherst was the impact on my teachers of the New Criticism. So I became excited, not only about the sort of literature to which the New Critics pointed, but also by the New Critics themselves and the idea of criticism. To think of looking at a poem and conveying what you see in it to a third person was very exciting. So I had an itch to be a scholar and critic when I was an undergraduate at Amherst, and when I was in graduate school at Harvard, and I would have been very sorry not to write some criticism, even after poetry and translation had more or less taken me over. Poe was someone I read as an adolescent—I suppose even younger than that—for the first time. During World War II I had among other things a beat-up little paperback of Poe in my knapsack; when I was in a foxhole at Monte Cassino, I started reading Poe and all of a sudden got a sense of submerged meaning in some of his stories: a very sure sense that it was there. Not that I knew what it was, but that it was there. So I began reading him with that conviction in mind. After the war, when I was at Harvard, had done my M.A. and decided not to go for the doctorate but be a junior fellow, I started reading Poe again—hard. And I wrote most of a book on Poe which I had to throw away because I was not able to find the right terms for describing what was going on underneath the surface. But I did teach a course in him at the time, and since then, once or twice, I've taught courses in him —always seminar-sized courses, so that everybody could mull freely and collectively and make discoveries. And now and then I've done an introduction, a job of editing, an essay.

NB: I read your introduction to the Laurel edition of Poe's poetry almost twenty years ago. Your discussion of Poe's fascination with Supernal Beauty has made a lot of sense to me and to my students. Without it, the tales become simply horror stories which illustrate the use of techniques like the unreliable narrator.

RW: Well, it always *is* interesting to talk about the narrators in Poe; but since Poe himself argued that all imaginative literature has undercurrents of meaning, I think it's too bad not to go for those undercurrents, even though it involves a lot of wild conjecture and subjectivity.

NB: What is the difference between writing poetry and writing prose? Is it easier for you to write prose?

RW: I suppose prose is an easier thing for me to write than verse, but both are hard for me. If your main business is writing poetry, you find it hard not to write a somewhat incrusted prose or, at any rate, a prose you've worried pretty hard. I write prose very slowly, just as I do verse. I think slowly, and write slowly, and I wish I were able to do what my wife does, which is write a damned good letter very fast and get it into the mail. I've never been able to kid myself into doing that, even by sticking the paper directly into the typewriter and hammering it out. Mostly I find myself, if it's a serious letter, writing a few notes in pencil before I ever get to the typewriter. That slows matters down. As I've confessed here and there, it's sometimes taken me five years to finish a poem. Fortunately, it's never taken me five days to finish a letter. *(Laughter.)*

NB: When you write prose, do you make notes or outline before you write?

RW: I don't outline. Well, I suppose I'd better not lie. Sometimes I have tried to outline, but I've never outlined before starting. I've always started, then discovered that I was in a mess, and then made a little list of what points I ought to make and in what order. That, I suppose, is an outline. I've never used the "I" and "A" and "B" and "C" kind of outline, but I have gone so far as to sketch a structure in the margin of the page to clarify the confusion I've gotten into.

NB: It sounds like you write prose the way you write poetry, just following . . .

RW: I just try to see which idea logically comes next. I don't know what the rule for the paragraph is, but I think I know what a paragraph is. *(Laughter.)*

NB: The student you mentioned who knew all the grammatical rules but couldn't use them is a wonderful example of why there's no point in learning those rules.

RW: The advantage to the rule is that if you're telling someone where he is wrong . . .

NB: You can identify it.

RW: That's why, when I teach a poetry writing course, I give the first day to talking about meters, rhymes and stanzas. I discuss all of the technical terms, and the point is not that the students will then know how to put five feet together and get a pentameter, but that when they're criticizing the poems I hand out at the next meeting, they'll be able to say: "There seems to be a foot lacking here." *(Laughter.)*

NB: What part of your education was most helpful to your writing?

RW: Certain of my literature courses presented me excitingly with writing which made me want to "do something like that." The same is true of the courses I've taught. The courses most useful to me have been the ones which excited me by putting me into the presence of things which I wanted not so much to copy as to equal in art and vitality.

NB: If there had been a lot of writing programs around when you were a student, do you think it would have been a good idea for you to go to one?

RW: Probably not a good idea at all. I went to Amherst. Amherst is a place I'm terribly fond of, and so I shall probably exaggerate its virtues, but the air of Amherst is full of approval for poetry and for writing, and always has been. You can't solve the matter by saying, "Oh, Emily Dickinson lived in that town," or "Oh, Robert Frost was on the faculty for a while." It's no one thing, it's no number of things that you can add up, it's just there. There was a great deal of extra-curricular excitement about writing when I was a student there, and all of one's teachers were glad to look at anything in the way of a poem or a story and criticize it. They were always very encouraging, and with all that encouragement, it wasn't necessary to burrow into a writing course. A number of my friends did take the one writing course then offered at Amherst, but I didn't see the necessity. I visited it once; it seemed OK, but I felt I would learn more somewhere else.

NB: Some people have said that it hurts literature to have so many people become writers by going through writing programs.

RW: I think it's hurting a lot of people, and that it's hurting the whole scene. I'm not alone in having this cranky feeling. Too many people are failing to study what they *should* study by concentrating too much on creative writing courses. There are so many schools in which people are allowed to major in creative writing, right through to a B.A. They go through impoverished, knowing, as Yeats said, "nothing but their blind, stupified hearts." And so often, having become defective and specialized in this way, they go on to graduate school in creative writing, and then drift on out into the M.F.A. market looking for jobs, not too many of which are there. Until recently, the government has been providing them with poetry in the schools programs, occasional fellowships and subsidized little magazines in which they can publish. It's a lamentably "supportive" world in which far too many people are encouraged to imagine themselves poets beyond the point at which they should wake up and decide to do something useful. One consequence of all this overencouragement and subsidizing is that we have quantities of little magazines full of bad poetry, depressing poetry, around us. Standards are lowered as soon as you have a whole lot of creative writing courses, because you can't ask for the highest performance of young people who have not had much experience as writers and have no strong calling. Insensibly, you lower your standard. And standards are lowered on the graduate level, because there are so many people going to these competing schools of writing. I think that the cessation or lessening of government support for poetry is not going to be a bad thing. I have no desire to make anybody stop writing poetry, but I think it would be a favor to many people and to poetry if some people stopped thinking of themselves primarily as young poets and kept on writing on the side.

It affects everybody if a whole lot of bad work in any art is being published and supported. If there are magazines all around us full of poems which start, "I turn off the television," and so on—that sort of loose-jointed, prosaic, supposedly sincere poem that says what you have done in the last five minutes—it's going to affect the general sense of what poetry ought to be doing.

NB: I'd like to ask about "The Writer," the poem you wrote to your daughter. What did you mean by "It is always a matter of life . . . and death"?

RW: Getting oneself off one's chest, writing. I'm wishing her a lucky passage, and it's a passage both in the sense of making connections with the world, getting out of oneself, and of writing a good paragraph. When one is dealing with young writers, one almost always has both those feelings going: you're hoping that the young writer will do well, will write a good story or a good poem; you're also hoping that the doing of that will be a successful coming to terms with the world by way of the common means of language.

NB: Is there anything you'd like to add?

RW: Yes. Since many of my remarks have been a bit negative or tart, I'd like to right the balance by saying that there is, in fact, much good poetry being written these days, that year after year I encounter students who are truly gifted, and that a course in writing can be stimulating and salutary. As for anyone's taking *two* such courses, or three, at the cost of neglecting Geology or Latin, I have my doubts.

HELEN YGLESIAS

NB: I was sorry that I couldn't get a copy of Starting. *Is that an autobiographical book?*

HY: *Starting* is nonfiction; about doing what you really want to do; especially women, I think, get sidetracked.

It does have a section on myself; as soon as I started to read, to be able to tell a story seemed to me the most wonderful thing to do, but I did not get to do it until I was fifty-four. I was editing and working on newspapers and magazines and even that work was interrupted because I had three children I wanted to raise myself, so I didn't go back to work full-time—I did things in between: I did free-lance editing and free-lance reviewing and so on—but I didn't go back to full-time work in the field, I'm not even talking about *writing* full-time, until my youngest child was ten or eleven. By that time I had pretty much given up the idea of writing fiction. I was a book editor on a weekly magazine. As a reader, I had been reading only the top novels. When you're a book editor you see everything. A lot of mediocre stuff is published. That was a big revelation: all this material was being published, being hailed, in some cases, as wonderful, as works of genius—some works that I thought were pretty bad. It leveled my sights. I said to myself, "Write the best book you can and see what happens." I wrote *How She Died.* And I was very, very fortunate.

My oldest son, who was then in his early twenties, picked up the manuscript and read the first chapter without my knowing it because I don't like to show things that aren't finished. He suggested that it would stand alone as a short story, which was something I couldn't have seen because I was too involved in it as a whole book, and that I should send it to *The New Yorker.* My husband had published in *The New Yorker,* and so it seemed natural to send it to his editor. It was taken, and its editor, a marvelous woman, Rachel MacKenzie, sent it to Houghton Mifflin to another wonderful editor, Dorothy de Santillana, who immediately offered me the Houghton Mifflin Literary Fellowship. That was overwhelmingly encouraging. I trusted myself then.

I wrote *Starting* because I felt my own experience could be encouraging to other people, and in *Starting,* I also tell stories of other people, not necessarily all late starters. As a matter of fact, I tell the story of my son who was a very early starter: he had a book published at seventeen.

NB: I came to these interviews with prejudices about artists that I'd picked up from reading Freud and Jung: that you all create because you're neurotic and so forth. You all seem so much healthier . . .

HY: *(Laughter.)* Than you expected.

NB: And than academics, or normal people. I think you're better able to follow yourselves.

HY: You have to be very strong to be a writer. This quote is from a wonderful Czech writer, Vaculik: "Writing is always somehow an expression of powerlessness, or the fruit of frayed nerves. It betrays complexes, or a bad conscience." I think that's true; but to write also takes a lot of ego strength and ego health. Otherwise, it's just too hard to pull it out of yourself.

Fiction, for me, is an immersion in the world I'm creating. It absorbs my total energy; I'm lucky if there's anything left over for the people who are closest and dearest to me. My reaction to a student's manuscript on my desk when I'm involved in my own work is, "I don't care about this, I don't want to read this." I don't even care to read published fiction when I'm writing. I will reread, or I'll read some classic that I haven't gotten to, but I won't read contemporary fiction. In fact, I get so crazy when I'm writing something, everything seems to relate to what I'm writing. My reaction to almost any book by almost any other contemporary woman writer is, "Oh, she's writing exactly what I'm writing!" It's that syndrome you experience when you learn something new and then see the new thing everywhere.

I find it very difficult to teach and write at the same time: I have to feel the entire day is mine for my own work. At Columbia it was set up so that [I taught] only one day in the week, and even then it was as though I had opened myself up to inroads on my own imaginative energy. Once I had done that, I couldn't turn off the rest of the week. I also have to feel I'm in my own space; even though this is my private office, in my mind, it's associated with the teaching.

NB: Why do you teach?

HY: I didn't know why the first time. I taught at Columbia after I wrote *How She Died* thinking I could start to write *Family Feeling* while I was teaching. I don't think I wrote three lines during that spring semester.

NB: Then why did you come here to teach?

HY: I had just finished *Sweetsir,* a novel which was very draining. After I complete a book, perhaps not everybody goes through this, but I need a period of recuperation and filling up again. While I was still working on *Sweetsir,* the request to teach at Iowa came in and I thought, "I'll be through with this novel and it will be nice to do something that won't take anything out of me." I had totally forgotten how demanding teaching is. I taught the other class in the mid-seventies. I like teaching and I enjoyed that experience. I made good friends among the students; I was instrumental in getting one of them published and I was very happy about that. I remembered it through a haze of good feeling as having been a lovely time. Now that I'm in the situation again it's coming back to me [that] I get very wound up in teaching.

I like young people very much; I have three children and two grandchildren; I don't mean that I relate to the students as a mother or a grandmother. I don't. I relate to them as someone who has the same difficulties they have. It's as if there's almost no time span between me now and me at age twenty thinking, "Oh, I want to be a writer; I want to be a writer; I can't wait." I don't feel separated from that person. I still feel something wonderful and miraculous happened to me that I pulled through and got published. So I identify very strongly with the feeling of a beginning writer. I think you have the sensation of beginning again with each new book; you feel after you complete a book, "I don't know how I did that: I'll never be able to do that again."

I get very involved in student manuscripts and in conferring with the writer. The students I've been in contact with are graduate students and they're screened and they're talented and they're serious. They're not all going to make it, but there are enough who *could* make it that I get very concerned for them and try to help them as much as I can. A very varied personality structure goes into making writers, naturally; they're like all other people. The single thing writers have in common is the desire to write or the need to write or the compulsion to write. And to be so closely involved with so many writers in the most basic relationship, judging what they're doing, affects me in a way that I can't throw off easily. I'm sure I would if I taught regularly. It would become routine, but I wouldn't particularly care for that. It is possible to read manuscripts absolutely coldly, but not if you're going to be of any help. To be of help, you have to immerse yourself in the particular imagination at work in that story; that's the only way you can see where it's gone wrong —or right.

Here we teach a workshop that has fifteen, sixteen people in it and that's much too large. You can't easily know sixteen people and what they're working on and have real entrance into their talent and their minds.

NB: How many students did you have at Columbia?

HY: We had eight; exactly half. The class was actually ten, but one never showed and there'd be a fluctuating member. Generally, at each seminar there would be eight. Eight is manageable; fifteen, sixteen is not. The workshop tends to be unbalanced by those who are forceful, those who take over. I worry about the ones who aren't speaking up, who aren't making themselves felt, particularly because writers are not always very articulate. Some very good writers are very inarticulate.

Writers project themselves into the feelings of others. When you are that sort of person, it's hard to be in contact with a roomful of suffering personalities. I project onto them how I would feel in that situation and I know I would be suffering agonies. I never took such a class because I would have found it too painful to expose a work that is not totally finished, that has not reached the stage where I feel, "Yes, I am ready to show this."

At the same time, you don't want to overprotect. You want to do your job which is to show where the writer has failed, and where the writer has succeeded. But what you know that the beginning writer doesn't know is that your views are essentially meaningless individual reactions. After a writer has been accepted and published, he or she is reviewed across the board. One person is going to say, "It's great" and someone at the other end is going to say, "It's garbage" and the writer finds the way within that. The exposure aspect is very painful to a writer, but to a professional, it's part of the scene and there are other bolstering aspects feeding in. I worry about a workshop being damaging to a beginning writer. I would not want anyone to leave my workshop feeling, "Well, I don't want to write anything. The last thing I want to do right now is write another story for them to get their teeth into." That's not the purpose of a workshop. All of that grips me in a way that I can't throw off lightly.

NB: How do you teach? It sounds as if you lose yourself in what they're trying to do.

HY: I try to stay totally within the text. On one level, a teacher operates as an example; you use yourself, your experience as a writer, your aims as a writer and your work where you can, to illustrate what you're saying. But in a more precise way, I operate as an editor because I do have that experience. I work closely with the text and try very hard not to change the story. Very often the students in the class are saying to a writer, "Don't write that story; write this story; I like this story better." They make up a totally different story which doesn't interest the writer one bit. What interests him is, "How can I make *this* story a better story." I stay very close to the text, and try to demonstrate skills. There *are* real skills. It's not all inner wisdom. Many of my writing friends and acquaintances have taught writing at one time or another, and many of them have said to me, "You cannot teach writing." If their approach to fiction is that it cannot be taught, then they're wrong to teach it. I don't mean you can teach someone how to become a first-rate writer or a great writer;

I don't think you can teach that. We're not talking about that. We're talking about professionalism; we're talking about preparing the story at the level where it can go out to a magazine and be read and judged and possibly bought; we're talking about preparing the novel to a point where it can be considered by a publishing house. It is true that there are writers who never need that; they have read enough to have learned the trade without these crutches. Most people who turn to writing classes do so because they have some problem or another: it may be only a problem of not having the self-discipline to do the work. That's a perfectly valid reason for taking a writing course. Or simply a need to meet other writers.

NB: You never took a course like this, but I assume you went to college.

HY: No, I never went to college. I've taken the equivalent of what any college student would have taken in English Literature courses which I monitored without credit. When you pick and choose that way, you're probably getting better instructors. I don't think writers need formal education as writers. It's very good for writers to be something else in their lives; it's wonderful that Chekhov was a doctor, for example. Even though living my life and working at what I worked at and having children and raising them kept me from writing, it also made it possible for me to have something very solid to write about when I did begin to write. One thing I don't like about a lot of contemporary writing is that it isn't about anything; there's a lot of emptiness at the center, particularly the writing by very young people that comes out of writing workshops. They want to be writers, but they don't have subjects.

A lot of writing is about writers in publishing or on magazines or it's about writers who teach. It's not about the people who are out there leading what we like to think of as ordinary lives but which aren't the least bit ordinary. They're very extraordinary. One of the critical reviews I got of *How She Died,* which was in the main praised, criticized it for taking what he considered very ordinary people and trying to make them extraordinary. He's a leading academic critic and his reaction is typical. If it couldn't happen in the back pages of the *New York Review of Books,* it's not worthy of our attention.

NB: What do you think it does to writing when so many people who write are associated with universities in one way or another?

HY: I think it's not good for writing. I think it's good stylistically; they're writing very well-made stories and their surface is very beautiful. A lot of them get into *The New Yorker.* I say that though I've gotten in myself at least twice. Nevertheless, there is such a thing as a typical *New Yorker* story which I find empty in its core, and I don't think that's wonderful for writing. Or for readers.

Books should be well-crafted and well-written, but novels should be about more than the closed world of the university or the closed world of publishing: about only middle-class, privileged people: or about the older professor who is having an affair with a beautiful young student; or the older wife of the older professor having an affair. I don't want to read any more of those books.

NB: I was struck by the power of the details you used in How She Died, *and since my father died of cancer, I know they were accurate. I was going to ask you how you did that, but I think you've already told me: you didn't write that book when you were 25 years old.*

HY: It's a made-up book: the character Jean is not me and has no relationship to my life except in that every character you write is yourself. But the character of the girl who died is very closely based on a dear friend and on her actual experience.

NB: Can you teach students how to select details that work the way yours do?

HY: The Orwell essay, "Why I Write," is wonderful; it's a plea for concrete language. It's a good antidote to the theory that it's all in the language; it's all in the surface; it's all the play of the language; it's all in the puns and the jokes. That is not even true of Joyce. There is solidity in *Ulysses;* there's reality behind the paratactics, and if you put it all onto the paratactics, you come up with nothing. You come up with razzle dazzle.

At the opening session, one of my students said he had come to my class because he felt that I would stress feeling and concrete experience in writing, whereas, other writing classes had stressed technique: structure, style. I reminded him that you can't do the feeling and experience without the structure and the style. They are totally interlocked, and must be granted equal weight and space. A writer works to give the reader a true experience and, yes, to dazzle while doing it. Orwell aims for a style that is as clear as a pane of glass so that there is no obstruction between the text and the reader. That's the major lesson I try to impart. That it is clarity which makes for the purest, brightest dazzle: clarity — and content.

WRITERS INTERVIEWED

Marvin Bell is on the poetry faculty of the Iowa Writers' Workshop. His recent books include *These Green-Going-To-Yellow; Old Snow Just Melting: Essays and Interviews;* and *Segues: A Correspondence in Poetry* (with William Stafford).

Kelly Cherry, who teaches at the University of Wisconsin-Madison, has published poetry, fiction, and nonfiction; for instance: the poetry collection *Relativity* and the novels *In the Wink of an Eye* and *The Lost Traveler's Dream.*

Seymour Epstein is a fiction writer now on the faculty of Denver University; his most recent novels are *Looking for Fred Schmidt* and *Love Affair.*

Allen Ginsberg, a co-founder of the Jack Kerouac School of Disembodied Poetics at the Naropa Institute, has written *Howl, Kaddish, The Fall of America,* and *Plutonian Ode: Poems 1977–1980.* He is a Guggenheim fellow, a member of the American Institute of Arts and Letters and has received the National Book Award.

Clarence Major is currently on the faculty of the University of Colorado at Boulder. He has published twelve books, among them the poetry collection *Swallow the Lake,* and the novels *Emergency Exit* and *Reflex and Bone Structure.*

Frederick Manfred writes fiction and teaches at the University of South Dakota. He has published over twenty-five novels, including *Lord Grizzly, Conquering Horse, The Wind Blows Free,* and *Green Earth.*

James Alan McPherson received the Pulitzer Prize for *Elbow Room,* a collection of short stories. He is currently on the faculty of the Iowa Writers' Workshop.

N. Scott Momaday, who writes in many genres, was awarded the Pulitzer Prize for his novel, *House Made of Dawn.* He is now a member of the English Department at the University of Arizona.

Lisel Mueller won the American Book Award for one of her poetry collections, *The Need to Hold Still.* She has taught at Goddard College and Lake Forest College.

The poet **William Stafford** has retired from Lewis and Clark College, but continues to give workshops around the country. He received the National Book Award for *Traveling Through the Dark.* His latest books are *A Glass Face in the Rain: New Poems* and *Segues: A Correspondence in Poetry* (with Marvin Bell).

Wallace Stegner was associated with the writing program at Stanford University for over twenty years before his retirement. Since then, he has won the Pulitzer Prize for *Angle of Repose,* and the National Book Award for *The Spectator Bird.* Other recent books include: *American Places: Human, Natural, and Personal History* and *One Way to Spell Man.*

Diane Wakoski has been on the faculty of fifteen universities and is now at Michigan State University. She has written over twenty books of poetry, among them, *The Motorcycle Betrayal Poems, Cap of Darkness, The Man Who Shook Hands,* and *The Magician's Feastletters.*

Anne Waldman co-founded the Jack Kerouac School of Disembodied Poetics at the Naropa Institute and formerly directed the Poetry

Project at St. Mark's Church in New York City. Her books include *Fast Speaking Woman, First Baby Poems,* and *Make-Up on Empty Space.*

Theodore Weiss is a member of the English Department at Princeton University. He edits the *Quarterly Review of Literature* with his wife Renée, has written a book of criticism, *The Breath of Clowns and Kings: Shakespeare's Early Comedies and Histories,* and several collections of poetry, among them, *Gunsight, Views and Spectacles: Selected Poems, Fireweeds,* and *Recoveries.*

Richard Wilbur has received the Pulitzer Prize and the National Book Award for his poetry which is collected in some twenty books, including: *The Poems of Richard Wilbur, Walking to Sleep,* and *The Mind-Reader.* He teaches at Smith College.

Helen Yglesias has taught at Columbia University and the Iowa Writers' Workshop. Her novels are: *Sweetsir, Family Feeling,* and *How She Died,* for which she won the Houghton Mifflin Award. She has also written a nonfiction book: *Starting: Early Anew, Over, and Late.*